THE SMART GUIDE TO

Mastering eBay

BY MARCUS NIEVES

The Smart Guide To Mastering eBay

Published by

Smart Guide Publications, Inc.
2517 Deer Chase Drive
Norman, OK 73071
www.smartguidepublications.com

For information, address: Smart Guide Publications, Inc. 2517 Deer Creek Drive, Norman, OK 73071

SMART GUIDE and Design are registered trademarks licensed to Smart Guide Publications, Inc.

International Standard Book Number: 978-1-937636-06-7

Library of Congress Catalog Card Number:
11 12 13 14 15 10 9 8 7 6 5 4 3 2 1

Printed in the United States of America

Cover design: Lorna Llewellyn
Copy Editor: Ruth Strother
Back cover design: Joel Friedlander, Eric Gelb, Deon Seifert
Back cover copy: Eric Gelb, Deon Seifert
Illustrations: James Balkovek
Production: Zoë Lonergan
Indexer: Cory Emberson
V.P./Business Manager: Cathy Barker

ACKNOWLEDGEMENTS

I wish to give special thanks to my teachers who saw in me the ability to write while I was growing up. Among those who nurtured my writing was my college professor of creative writing—he was the first to ask if he could publish a story I wrote, which caused me to pursue writing seriously. I give special thanks to my publisher Frank Jerome and my literary agent Mary Sue Seymour. This book would not exist without them.

The very biggest thanks go to my mother, Carmen Rodriguez. Her support throughout my entire life made all of my accomplishments possible.

Finally, I would like to thank my son Marcus Jr. He is the inspiration for everything I have done in my career. He gives me the will and the drive to take on any task and to be the very best role model I can be.

Marcus Nieves
Orlando, FL

TABLE OF CONTENTS

INTRODUCTION

Have you always wondered what all the hype is about over eBay? Have you been curious about eBay but have been unwilling to use it without knowing more about it? Have you always dreamed about starting your own business? How about working from home? Well, you're in for a great adventure as you turn the pages of *The Smart Guide to eBay*. You will find guidance, tips, and resources in this book that will teach you the ins and outs of buying and selling on eBay.

You will start on the ground level and learn how to navigate through eBay and have some fun "window shopping." Then you will learn about the various ways you can buy on eBay, followed by how to sell and open an eBay store. So whether you're here just to play around or you're serious about opening an eBay store, these pages will walk you through the steps.

You will find it helpful to have a computer handy so you can follow along as you read through the steps. Don't be afraid to explore on your own as well. You'll notice that there is a lot of overlap on eBay and that you can get to the same nuggets of information from various links and various pages.

If a question comes up that this book doesn't answer, you're likely to find the answer somewhere on the eBay website. You'll find eBay's Learning Center particularly helpful.

As you read through *The Smart Guide to eBay* keep in mind that eBay is a dynamic enterprise; it is constantly changing and improving. The information in this book is accurate as of the writing of the book, but eBay will make changes to its site as time goes on. These changes will likely render some of the information herein obsolete. It's the nature of the Internet. So if information in this book doesn't quite mesh with what you're seeing on the eBay website, look for updates and answers at eBay's Learning Center.

Some eBay pages may look slightly different depending on if you're approaching them as a seller or as a buyer. And some seller pages may not be accessible to you if you're not registered as a seller. So if you're reading through the section on selling, you may want to take the plunge and register as a seller. Then you can go step-by-step with the book, as you did in the buying section, to create your listings and maybe even set up your eBay Store.

As you read through the book, you'll notice that there are sidebars peppered throughout the pages. The sidebars are included to highlight information that may be especially interesting or useful. You'll find three types of sidebars:

1. eBay Basics, which includes some basic aspects or functions of eBay

2. Helpful Tip, which gives you tips that will help you get even more out of eBay or will direct you to sources that will further your eBay knowledge

3. eBay Expressions, which defines terms or ideas associated with eBay

eBay has a lot to offer within its enormous website. After working your way through this book, you'll need to actually buy and sell to really get a feel for how eBay works. Once you have some transactions under your belt, though, you will be hooked. It's invigorating to be a part of this exciting and expanding network of buyers and sellers from around the world. Have fun with your explorations and welcome to your new adventure!

PART ONE

Registering

CHAPTER 1

In the Beginning

In This Chapter

➤ eBay Origins

➤ What Is eBay

➤ Types of auctions

➤ Rules of eBay

In this chapter you will be introduced to eBay, an online marketplace and auction site that has changed the way millions of people buy and sell all matter of goods. Other such sites exist, but eBay remains the reigning king of auction sites.

You will be introduced to how eBay got its start, what eBay can do for you, and what you can do on eBay. You'll get a rundown of topics that will be covered later in the book in greater detail. For now, welcome to eBay. I know you'll love it.

eBay Origins

On September 3, 1995, during a Labor Day weekend, Pierre Omidyar created what was soon about to become one of the biggest

eBay Basics

Rumor has it that eBay was supposed to be a tongue-in-cheek reference to Ebola since Auction Web, eBay's predecessor in name, was hosted by a website dedicated to educating people about Ebola. Official statements by Pierre Omidyar, however, claimed that he wanted to rename his web-based auction site Echo Bay after his consulting firm, but the domain name echobay.com had already been registered. So he shortened the name to eBay.

auction and e-commerce websites on the planet. Originally called Auction Web and hosted by a website dedicated to information on Ebola, eBay has spawned countless auction sites and many other prominent and prestigious sites since.

The first item ever sold on Auction Web was Omidyar's very own broken laser pointer. It sold for $14.83. Flabbergasted, Omidyar asked the buyer why he bought a broken laser pointer, to which the buyer replied that he was a collector. This was the start of what is now a billion dollar business.

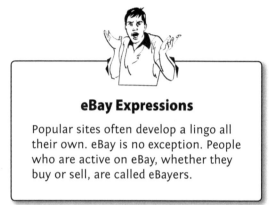

eBay Expressions

Popular sites often develop a lingo all their own. eBay is no exception. People who are active on eBay, whether they buy or sell, are called eBayers.

Today, eBay is nearly an entire world unto its own. The eBay community has its own etiquette, its own rules, even its own laws. There are millions of eBayers that have immersed themselves wholly into the site and buy and sell on eBay every day. These people treat it the way day traders treat the stock market, and rightly so. You will see how important it is to monitor not only your auctions, but your bids, especially if the item is rare or the right price or just something you really want.

Although the lion's share of this book will be about selling on eBay, buyers' demand is half of what makes the marketplace function. Without demand, after all, there would be no need for supply (and boy does eBay supply). Let's take a look at eBay from the buyer's point of view.

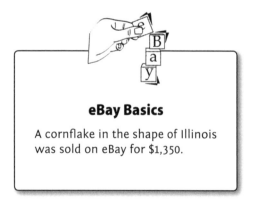

eBay Basics

A cornflake in the shape of Illinois was sold on eBay for $1,350.

One-Stop Shop

Many people speak of it, many websites refer to it, but I think very few people fully grasp the extent of the vast variety of items that can be sold and bought on eBay. I will bet that any single possible item you can think of, eBay has, has had, or will have a listing for, within its rules and regulations, that is. If you want an easy-to-find video game, you're likely to find it on eBay. If you are looking for a first edition of *Oliver Twist*, eBay may be your best bet.

I have seen people decorate their entire homes with purchases from eBay. People can buy a wardrobe for work, an engine part to get their SUVs running, or a kitchen appliance with which to cook dinner.

Even if you're shopping for everyday items, eBay may be a better resource than a brick-and-mortar store. Often, eBay merchants sell products comparable to that of a brick-and-mortar store at a significantly lower price. And you may end up with a great deal through bidding in an eBay auction.

Selling

Selling is what eBay is all about. Many people have decided to make eBay their supplemental or even primary form of income. Some people clean out their attics or garages of long-forgotten "treasures" and sell them on eBay as a way to make additional money. And some use eBay as a place to run a business that sustains 100 percent of the household income. Millions of eBayers are selling billions of dollars of items.

Anyone who tells you eBay is not a good venue for income or not a good way to start a business has clearly never seen eBay millionaires. Men and woman sell thousands of products a week on eBay. They have entire warehouses of inventory that they need to categorize, computerize, invoice, and record; in short, many who sell on eBay manage all the business aspects that would put some larger brick-and-mortar businesses to shame. eBay is one of the best things to happen to digital commerce.

What's to Come

The next levels of selling on eBay are becoming a PowerSeller, a top-rated seller, and owning an eBay store. Later in this book you will learn how to create your own eBay store, the basics you need to know to sustain such a business model, and how to help it flourish. You will also learn about the digital commerce payment system known as PayPal, as well as other methods of payment.

You will learn about eBay's feedback system, the part of eBay that makes shoppers feel safe purchasing from absolute strangers. Constantly imitated but never duplicated, the feedback system (often compared to a credit score) is one of the best parts of eBay. It keeps sellers honest, it gives buyers peace of mind, and it creates the difference between a now-and-again eBayer and a top-rated seller.

This book is written for readers who have never used eBay. Its step-by-step, detail-oriented format is geared toward the layperson who has not yet dabbled in what eBay has to offer. As such, this book will cover the eBay basics, but it can only touch upon all that eBay has to offer because, let's face it, eBay's myriad features would overflow just one book.

What is eBay?

eBay is an auction site dedicated to bringing people who have items to sell together with those who are looking for items to buy, with the items ranging from the hard-to-find that no store on earth could possibly have to the ordinary.

Many people have the common misconception that eBay is a store. Although eBay is a company and has shareholders and directors, the buying and selling is done by people like you and me. Millions of people put up their items for sale for others to buy; millions of people buy or bid on items that are for sale. There is no one store that you can walk into and actually see every single auction item. There is no eBay supercenter like Walmart. Each eBayer is completely independent.

There are several types of auctions that buyers and sellers can engage in. Let's take a brief look at those auctions.

Types of Auctions

Auctions on eBay have no auctioneer. I imagine if there were, eBay would have to have a few hundred thousand auctioneers working round the clock, and they'd all be suffering from chronic laryngitis. Instead, eBay auctions are completely time controlled. Whereas traditional auctions can be won and ended by a specific bid, eBay auctions usually start and stop at a specific time. In the typical eBay auction, the highest bidder at the moment the clock stops is deemed the winner. Let's run through the list of the different types of auctions.

Standard Auctions

Standard auctions are the typical time-based auctions. The seller places a minimum price on the item up for sale as a starting point for the bidding. I have seen auctions start as low as 1¢ and sell for 5¢. The flip side of standard auctions is that the sky's the limit. I have seen bidding wars break out on the most unlikely items and end with a record-breaking winning bid. These auctions are the very heart of eBay and have changed little since eBay's inception.

Reserve Price Auctions

In the standard auction, a seller sets a minimum price and lets the bidding commence. When the auction time runs out the seller parts with his or her item no matter what the winning bid is.

A seller can, however, set a reserve price—a secret price only the seller knows. Unless a bid reaches or surpasses that number, the item does not sell. Reserve price auctions are for sellers who have a minimum price in mind for the item.

Sometimes, though, the bidding doesn't reach that minimum price and the seller has to repost the item. So why doesn't the seller just begin the auction at the price he or she is seeking? You will come to learn the answer to that and similar questions when you learn about the many strategies of auctioning.

For the buyer's sake, the reserve price does not remain hidden forever. The listing continues to maintain the message that the reserve price has not been met until it is met, and then the message changes accordingly. Once the bidders know that the reserve has been met, they can decide how far they want to proceed from there.

Buy It Now Auctions

The Buy It Now auctions are a particular favorite of mine. In many cases, they do not have the potential to yield the huge bids that can come with standard auctions, but when running an eBay store and selling regular everyday retail items, nothing beats the speed of Buy It Now auctions to move merchandise.

A long time ago, Buy It Now auctions were reserved for established eBayers. Your everyday Joe couldn't just create an account and have the option to sell using the Buy It Now auction. Now, anyone can use this fantastic feature right off the bat.

Buy it Now auctions are also good for buyers. There are those who do not want to sit through a weeklong auction or have a bidding war over the item they want. They just want to buy it the cleanest, quickest way possible. It is a great feature all around.

Other Auctions

There are several other less-used auction types you may want to be aware of. Private auctions keep the bidders' user IDs confidential. I have yet to engage in an auction where I wanted my identity concealed. Then again, I have engaged in the next auction I am about to discuss, in which many might want their identity to be concealed. That next auction is restricted access.

Helpful Tip

eBay offers a variety of auctions. The main auctions are:

➤ Standard

➤ Reserve

➤ Fixed Price, or Buy It Now

➤ Multiple items, or Dutch

➤ Private

➤ Restricted-access

You'll need to choose the format that is best for you and the item you'll be selling.

Restricted-access auctions require all involved to be over eighteen years of age. There are safeguards eBay has in place to ensure the bidders are over eighteen. These listings, adult in nature, can be bid on only if you have submitted and verified a valid credit card.

Another auction type is the fixed-price auction, which is similar to the Buy It Now auction. All this and more will be covered when we cover selling.

Even Fun Places Have Rules

eBay is soon going to be your best friend, especially if you love shopping. It is going to be an even better friend if you are a seller wanting to supplement your income. But even friendship has limits and restrictions. eBay enforces its rules and regulations and will call you out immediately if you violate them.

Over the years, much like any company, eBay has changed its rules and regulations, what's allowed or disallowed, but the fundamentals have always been the same. It should go without saying that rocket launchers, anthrax, nuclear weapons, and the like cannot be sold on eBay.

You will probably find that there are some disallowed items that you may not even have thought about it. Here is a brief list of taboo items (while these may seem obvious, you would be surprised by how many people have conniptions when they find out these are not allowed):

> ➤ Alcohol: There are myriad reasons why this is an obvious no-no, not the least of which is the potential for children to obtain alcohol in an uncontrolled environment. Another reason is that one must possess a liquor license to sell alcohol in the United States. Outside the United States, alcohol may be sold and purchased on eBay International but are subject to local laws.

There are exceptions, however. One such exception is alcohol sold as a collector's item (thirty-year-old single malt Scotch, for instance), but even then there are a multitude of guidelines to follow. Wine, of course, is also allowed but subject to the same stern restrictions except in this case, it is necessary for the seller to have a wine or liquor license.

> ➤ Firearms: As a father, I find restricting the sale of firearms on eBay a good rule. There are, in fact, several auction sites that do sell guns, but eBay strictly prohibits fully functioning firearms, period. It does allow the buying and selling of certain firearm accessories, which you can look up on eBay's policy site.

> ➤ Human body parts: First—eww. Second—it is not legal anywhere in the United States to traffic in human body parts, no matter what. This is not an eBay law but a US law.

➤ Animals: eBay does not allow the sale of any type of live animal for obvious reasons. For one, it's nothing to lose a package with an inanimate item, but to lose an animal could result in the delivery of an animal who has starved to death. If you have the proper permit you may sell a feeder animal, but it must be listed as that.

➤ Obvious items: The sale of explosives, ingredients for explosives, drugs (illegal or otherwise), counterfeit bills, credit cards, or any other item that is obviously illegal are not allowed on eBay. If you can be imprisoned for possessing the item, it's a safe bet you can't post it on eBay.

➤ Controversial items: The First Amendment allows for the basic civil rights of all individuals. As a US citizen, a person has the right to say what he or she wants or to protest nonviolently. eBay, however, is a private business, not the government, and it has the right to refuse items that contribute to hate to be posted on its site.

If after all your research you post an item that ends up being against eBay regulations, the vigilant people at eBay will end your auction and send you an e-mail stating why you cannot post said item.

Like any business, eBay has a long and extensive list of rules and regulations. Rather than trying to plow through this list, I suggest you simply use the policy part of the website as a reference guide when you need it. But, for the most part, common sense guides eBayers more often than not.

Well, now that you've been introduced to eBay, let's dive into what it is actually all about. Fasten your seatbelts, it's going to be a—well, rather smooth ride; you're shopping from the comforts of your home, after all. Welcome to eBay!

CHAPTER 2

Getting Started

> ### In This Chapter
> ➤ How to begin your eBay experience
> ➤ How to register on eBay
> ➤ Creating a user name
> ➤ An introduction to PayPal

In this chapter you will be introduced to the process of creating your eBay identity. You will learn how to register, the rules for creating a user name and password, and the rules and regulations of becoming an eBay member.

In many ways, eBay is like other e-commerce sites, but it has an additional component that makes it unique: eBay has acquired a digital e-commerce website called PayPal. You will be introduced to PayPal in this chapter. Let's get started.

How to Begin

It would be great if you could simply start buying and selling products on eBay, but without rules and standards this sort of commerce could prove risky to all involved—even eBay itself. eBay acts as an intermediary between seller and buyer and as such, it has developed some security measures that make using its site as safe and trouble-free as possible. One of those security measures is requiring that everyone register before being allowed to make transactions within the site. So your first step to becoming an eBayer is to create an account.

Creating an eBay account is not much different from registering on other e-commerce websites, but eBay uses some extra precautions. Its rules and regulations help ensure buyer security so there is no reason to heed the warning *caveat emptor,* and they help ensure that sellers do not get scammed out of their property by uncouth buyers.

eBay Expressions

Caveat emptor means "let the buyer beware" in Latin. The phrase means that a buyer takes the risk of purchasing an item without a warranty. The buyer, alone, is responsible for assessing the quality of the product and of the transaction.

Like most e-commerce sites, eBay provides a standard level of encryption so that your information is guaranteed to be safe on eBay's servers. eBay is a very secure site in which to conduct business and PayPal is an ultra-secure digital payment site.

Helpful Tip

You don't need to register before browsing through eBay's offerings. You can look at any item you please and even take a moment to see if eBay has anything you may want. Don't be shy. Look at sellers, look at auctions, compare prices, see what's on eBay. Treat yourself to virtual window shopping and look at the tool set you've been wanting or the Louis Vuitton bag you've been drooling over. Believe me, it is just as satisfying as walking through a half-mile mall wandering from window to window, the difference being that eBay has millions of items. What mall can boast that?

Setting Up

The very first step to setting up an account in any website is registering so that you may log into the website whenever you want to use it. Registering on eBay is fairly routine as website registration goes. Let's assume you are a newcomer and begin the registration process for eBay.

We'll start with the obvious, clicking the Register link in the upper left corner, which will take you to a Register with eBay page. Figure 2.1 shows a screenshot of the registration screen.

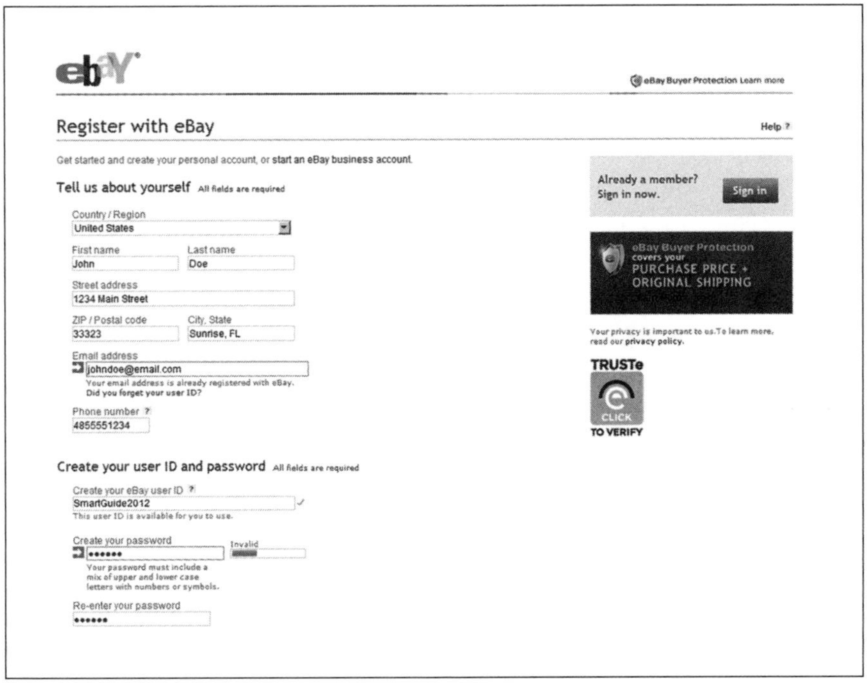

Figure 2.1

As you can see, you will be asked to input your personal information. This is important for myriad reasons, not the least of which is that you are entering into a legal and binding contract involving commerce, credit cards, and money. The Register with eBay page requires the following information:

> ➤ Supply your name
>
> ➤ Supply your address
>
> ➤ Supply your e-mail address
>
> ➤ Supply your phone number
>
> ➤ Create your eBay user ID, or screen name
>
> ➤ Create a password
>
> ➤ Select your secret question from the drop-down menu

➤ Provide your secret answer

➤ Fill in your date of birth

Choosing a user ID, or screen name, is an important first step in the eBay registration process. Your screen name will be your business name, the name you want people to remember when they shop. It will be what identifies and defines you.

Watch Your Mouth

Many people have a sense of humor or at the very least a sense of individuality that they insist on conveying through clever user names. It's best to keep a few things in mind when creating a screen name, especially if you plan to play in an arena where you wish to make money:

➤ Avoid profanity: First off, eBay has rules against profanity. That aside, no matter how funny you find a coarse user name or how much it reflects you or your individuality, names that you wouldn't say in a G-rated movie should be avoided.

➤ Don't be offensive: Choose a name that won't turn business away, especially if you plan to make money through this venue. As an analogy, I play a lot of online war games. It is frowned upon to team kill, but there are many players who do in fact choose names such as Best Team Killer as a prank. In the same vein, if you choose a name like Maxed Out Credit Card, even if it is a funny inside joke referring to how often you shop, it will most definitely make people wonder if you can pay for the goods. Consider what your name looks like from a stranger's standpoint.

➤ Invoke trust: If you are serious about doing business on eBay, you might want to consider using a screen name that invokes trust in a business environment and leave individuality, puns, or neat turns of phrases for a more casual situation. Your screen name is the first and possibly only thing people will know about you. Do you want it to be something that makes people uneasy? If so, see you on the welfare line.

➤ Keep user name and password distinct: Do not choose a user name that may be in any way part of your password. Although your password is in those neat little asterisks and you think no one can hack you, think again.

Passwords

After you create your unique screen name, you must create a password that consists of six to twenty characters, including letters, numbers, and symbols. Your password should not be related to your name, your user ID, or anything that can be associated with you or easy to guess.

Helpful Tip

Many people have a false sense of security where eBay and PayPal are concerned. They feel so safe that they don't see the importance of creating a hard-to-hack password. The fact is that companies are well-protected. The danger is the ease with which a person could hack you. You know those silly little viruses that your fabulous antivirus software blocks so easily? Well, all it takes is one of those little suckers to slip through, then bam! Your PayPal account is cleaned out.

Make your password as difficult as possible, despite the inconvenience of trying to remember a complicated string of characters.

After you've created a password, you'll be asked to choose a security question from a drop-down menu and to supply the corresponding answer. In case you forget your password, you can answer the security question to verify your identity. Make sure you choose a security question that is pertinent to you or that you will remember. You do not want to choose a security question that asks for your favorite author if you do not read much or one that asks what your favorite TV show is if you have seventeen favorite shows.

Once you fill in your date of birth you can hit the Submit button. By registering, you are agreeing to the following:

➤ You have read and accepted the user agreement and privacy policy

➤ You are amenable to receiving communications from eBay (you can always change your notification preferences in My eBay).

➤ You are at least eighteen years old.

It behooves you to read through the user agreement and private policy. After all, you are entering into a contract that is legally binding.

Once you've hit the Submit button, eBay will send you an e-mail. Follow the directions in the e-mail to activate your account. You are now an official eBayer.

eBay's Best Pal

You're not quite done yet, though. You must create a PayPal account whether you want to buy or sell an item. For that, it is essential you know a little about PayPal and e-commerce.

Aside from building a billion-dollar business from scratch, the CEO and eBay's board made what is, in my opinion, probably the greatest move in e-commerce history: they acquired PayPal, the payment system that has been associated with eBay for years. The acquisition resulted in simplifying eBay transactions and increasing eBay's revenue to an insane degree.

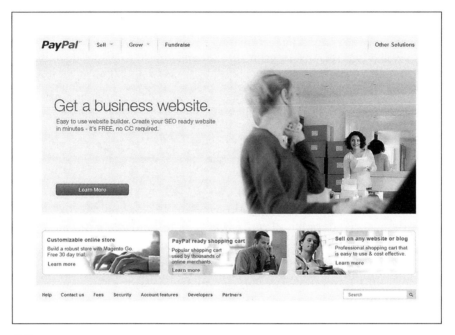

Figure 2.2

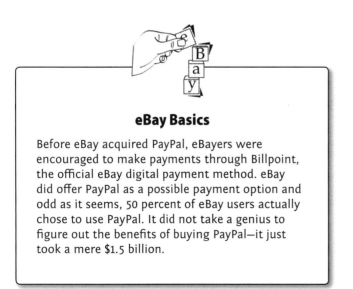

eBay Basics

Before eBay acquired PayPal, eBayers were encouraged to make payments through Billpoint, the official eBay digital payment method. eBay did offer PayPal as a possible payment option and odd as it seems, 50 percent of eBay users actually chose to use PayPal. It did not take a genius to figure out the benefits of buying PayPal—it just took a mere $1.5 billion.

PayPal was founded in 1998, the same year eBay went public. PayPal competed with eBay's own e-commerce auction payment system called Billpoint. PayPal eventually became the number one payment choice for an amazing 50 percent of all eBayers. In 2002, after years of eBay watching 50 percent of its auction payment revenue going to PayPal, eBay tendered an offer of $1.5 billion to PayPal, thus earning 100 percent of its auction payment fees. The acquisition of an online payment company by a company that uses online payments is simply genius, however obvious or inevitable a move like that might seem.

PayPal is now the digital payment method on eBay, not to mention the largest on the Internet. It is the quickest and most reliable payment method to date—even more reliable than credit cards. PayPal offers many features that provide security as well as speed.

Treat PayPal as you do your bank account, your credit cards, or any other medium that controls your finances. If you create a successful eBay store, you could have thousands of dollars going in and out of your PayPal account every day. So while you may be haphazard about other aspects of your business, I strongly advise you to protect your PayPal account with all the security measures available to you.

The basics of eBay registration are now in order and you are on your way to becoming a top-rated seller. But before you jump straight into eBay commerce, it's a good idea to learn more about PayPal. After all, you'll be entrusting your every dime, your every transaction, and, if you care to use PayPal in other ways, a significant part of your funds to PayPal. The next chapter will help you learn all about what PayPal can do for you.

CHAPTER 3

Pay with Your Pal

In This Chapter

➤ Setting up your PayPal

➤ Another Home page

➤ Choose your poison

➤ More rules

In this chapter you will become acquainted with a powerful and important part of eBay, possibly even of all of e-commerce. Getting to know the website that will be responsible for retaining any and all funds earned or spent on eBay gives just a little incentive to look that site over from beginning to end, inside and out. You will also learn what features it has and some of the ways to make it work efficiently for you.

PayPal Uses

PayPal allows you to pay or get paid quickly and safely without the need for you to share your financial information with whomever you're doing business with, whether a merchant, client, or employer. All you need to do is link your credit card, debit card, or bank account to your PayPal account, and then choose how you prefer to pay or get paid for goods or services. PayPal is safe, reliable, and it acts as an intermediary should either party behave in an unprofessional manner.

eBay Basics

As of 2012, you can find PayPal in 190 regions of the world, accepting twenty-four different world currencies, and providing services to over 84 million people.

We're focusing on the use of PayPal when making transactions on eBay, but it's worth noting that PayPal can be used with other websites, to pay or bill for services, even to make utility payments.

Registering with PayPal may take a few minutes and account verification may take a few days, but going through the process is well worth it for time saved in the future and the peace of mind that comes with transaction speed and safety.

Setting Up PayPal

PayPal takes rigorous steps during registration to ensure your account is safe and secure. Like any other site, once you register you'll never have to go through the process again. To begin, go to www.paypal.com and click on the Sign Up button. Figure 3.1 is a screenshot of the page that opens.

Figure 3.1

As you can see there are three options:

> ➤ Personal: For those who intend to shop online.

> ➤ Premier: For those who intend to buy and sell online. This is the best option if you plan to open an eBay store.

> ➤ Business: For merchants with a business name. These merchants must already have a company bank account.

PayPal will allow you to upgrade your account, so if you open a personal account today, you can always upgrade to a premier or business account when necessary.

After you have chosen the account you want, choose your country or region and language from the drop-down menu, and then click on the Get Started button. Figure 3.2 is a screenshot of the page that opens. Fill in the boxes, read the user agreement, privacy policy, acceptable use policy, and the electronic communications delivery policy, and then click on the Agree and Create an Account button.

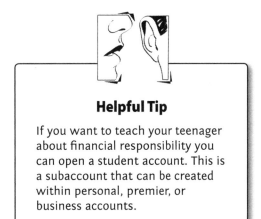

Helpful Tip

If you want to teach your teenager about financial responsibility you can open a student account. This is a subaccount that can be created within personal, premier, or business accounts.

PayPal

Enter your information   Secure

Please fill in all fields.

Email address
You will use this to log in to PayPal

Choose a password

Re-enter password

Legal first name

Legal last name

Address line 1

Address line 2 (optional)

City/State

ZIP code

Phone Why is this needed?
Type   Country Code Phone number
Mobile ▾ 1 (US) ▾

Add another phone number

☐ Yes, I've read and agree to the following:
  • PayPal's User Agreement, Privacy Policy, and Acceptable Use Policy.
  • The Electronic Communications Delivery Policy. I understand that PayPal will provide me with information about my account electronically. I confirm that I can access emails, web pages, and PDF files.

Agree and Create Account

Figure 3.2

Helpful Tip

Your e-mail address is the user name you'll use to log into your PayPal account. For added security, I recommend that you create a unique e-mail address to be used just with your PayPal account. And make sure to choose a password that can't be hacked.

Whatever you do, be honest about the information you supply to PayPal. If you are not who you say you are and falsify anything in the least, it can be considered a computer financial crime.

The next screen that pops up is shown in figure 3.3. It offers two ways of handling your account: by bank account or by credit or debit card. The credit or debit card method is intended for buyers, those who will be using PayPal in lieu of their credit or debit card.

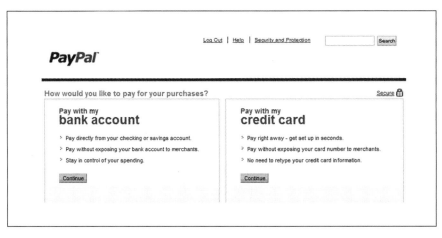

Figure 3.3

The bank account option is geared to those who intend to use eBay to its fullest extent, including those who plan to open an eBay store. You're reading this book to learn the ins and outs of eBay buying and selling, so you'll want to click on the Continue button under Bank Account Details. Figure 3.4 shows the next screenshot.

How would you like to pay for your purchases?   Secure 🔒

Pay with my
bank account

› Pay directly from your checking or savings account.

› Pay without exposing your bank account to merchants.

› Stay in control of your spending.

This bank account will become the default way to pay for most of
your transactions. You can select a preferred way to pay each time
you make a payment. View PayPal policies and your payment source
rights.

Bank name

Account type
⊙ Checking
○ Savings

Routing number
(9 digits) is usually located between the ⑆ symbols on your check.

Account number
Typically comes before the ⑈ symbol. Its exact location and number
of digits (3-17) varies from bank to bank.

Re-enter account number

U.S. Check Sample

⑆ 923456789 ⑆ 923456789 ⑈ 1234

Routing Number Account Number

Continue   Back

Figure 3.4

As you can see, the information that PayPal requires is directly connected to your bank. While this is incredibly safe given the encryption both PayPal and your bank uses, I strongly urge everyone to treat this information like any other financial and/or bank information. Never give anyone any of the information you see in figure 3.4 unless you and that person have said "I do" to each other and have exchanged rings. This information is top secret.

PayPal has a method to ensure that the bank information you entered is authentic. It deposits a small amount in your bank account (don't get excited, it's only somewhere between 3¢ and 5¢). The deposits take two to three business days to appear on your account. You will then

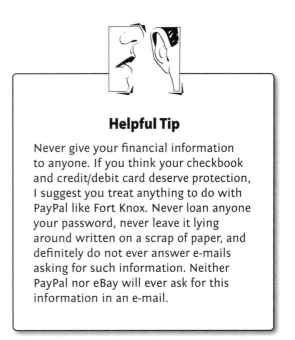

Helpful Tip

Never give your financial information to anyone. If you think your checkbook and credit/debit card deserve protection, I suggest you treat anything to do with PayPal like Fort Knox. Never loan anyone your password, never leave it lying around written on a scrap of paper, and definitely do not ever answer e-mails asking for such information. Neither PayPal nor eBay will ever ask for this information in an e-mail.

confirm with PayPal that you indeed received these deposits and, voilà! You are verified and your PayPal account is activated. You're on your way to becoming an eBay store owner and maybe even a top-rated seller. Good fortune!

PayPal's Home Page

Like eBay (and virtually every website on the Internet), PayPal directs you to the home page after you log in for the first time and every time after that. Once you log in, you are taken to your home base, the My Account Overview page shown in figure 3.5. From here, you can navigate to any part of PayPal. Let's run through the tabs in this home page.

Figure 3.5

My Account

The My Account page is your home base. You can view the transactions you've made recently, the payments sent, and the payments received. You can print shipping labels to people you've recently sold to and see who has paid you and who hasn't. Your My Account page has several tabs you should get comfortable with; some you will use frequently, others rarely.

➤ Overview: The main page of My Account.

➤ Add money: The link that takes you to the page that allows you to add funds to your PayPal account, presumably to make more purchases.

➤ Withdraw: Always a favorite, this page allows you to transfer the digital money on your screen to cash money in your hands

➤ History: Your record-keeping page, which lists all your past dealings sorted out in a time frame you choose (for example, Feb 2011–May 2011). You can alter it to show all activity, or you can be more specific and choose payments received, payments sent, or more filters. This page is undoubtedly invaluable for the sake of bookkeeping.

➤ Statements: You can download recent statements (similar to the statements banks send to you) in PDF format. Unfortunately, this page keeps records for only the past three months. It is a good idea to print out this page every month, and keep the hard copy for your files. Uncle Sam gets very interested in income that isn't claimed, and you definitely do not want to hear that dreaded word, *audit*.

➤ Resolution center: When a problem involving PayPal arises, such as not receiving a purchased item or not receiving payment for a purchased item, you can turn to PayPal's resolution center. If you have any sort of grievance, PayPal acts as mediator. It looks at all the available information and evidence regarding the two claims in question and makes a ruling. PayPal is fair and impartial and usually makes the right decision.

➤ Profile: Here you can customize and change your personal information and PayPal settings.

The Other Home Page Tabs

Besides My Account, you'll want to familiarize yourself with the other tabs along the top of PayPal's Home page. Here's the rundown:

➤ Send money: This tab allows you to send money online to anyone and specifically to pay for eBay items.

➤ Request money: Here you can manage invoices, request money, create invoices, and adjust your invoice settings.

➤ Merchant services: For the sake of thoroughness and to learn every possible way to conduct an e-commerce business, familiarize yourself with this link. This page includes subtabs labeled Solutions, Industries, Partners, and Resource Center. Each subtab has its own list of links that will direct you to pages filled with a wealth of information related to PayPal's merchant services.

➤ Products and services: You can skim through the wide variety of products and services PayPal has to offer, such as applying for a PayPal debit and/or credit card, viewing PayPal-approved discounts at retail stores, and shopping online at PayPal-approved retail outlets.

Depositing and Withdrawing

PayPal gives you some options for funding and withdrawing money from your account whether you are making purchases or selling items.

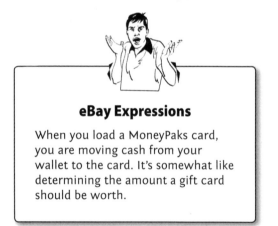

eBay Expressions

When you load a MoneyPaks card, you are moving cash from your wallet to the card. It's somewhat like determining the amount a gift card should be worth.

Funding

Besides relying on your bank account, you can add money to your PayPal account by using MoneyPaks, a prepaid card that can be purchased for $4.95 or less at participating retailers such as Walgreens and 7-Eleven. You load the card with funds, anywhere from $20 to $500 at most retailers, and use it to add money to your PayPal account (thus circumventing the need for a bank account) or make payments to other companies. The funds are available instantly.

Withdrawals

There are many ways to move funds out of PayPal, whether it is simply to withdraw the money in the form of cash or to transfer it. There are also more features available that may offer methods that could assist you in ways normal e-commerce accounts cannot.

➤ PayPal debit card: This is a versatile card similar to a prepaid debit card. Like a prepaid debit card, you can spend only the funds that it contains, so there is no way to go over and no way to be charged overdraft fees. Many people use the PayPal debit card to shop online. Nearly every single online commerce website accepts PayPal just as if it were a credit card.

The PayPal card is a great method of accessing your funds, it is protected just like any credit card, it is versatile, and the funds you obtain through the sale of an auction item on eBay are immediately available after the buyer's funds are verified.

The most common way to obtain funds with the PayPal card is by ATM withdrawal. Once you get your PayPal card, you can use it to withdraw funds at any ATM. You will be charged $1.00 by PayPal, and you'll have to pay any ATM fees that are required. You must have a confirmed bank account to be issued a PayPal debit card.

➤ Bank account: If you already have a confirmed bank account, transferring funds from your PayPal account to your bank account takes a few business days, but it is completely free. Being able to transfer money from your PayPal account to your business bank account so you can pay employees or pay yourself is important, and PayPal makes it easy.

➤ PayPal Check: The PayPal check is for those people who do not have a confirmed bank account or PayPal debit card. Withdrawing money by requesting a PayPal check can take a considerable amount of time. PayPal charges a $1.50 check-writing fee for this service.

Rules, Rules, and More Rules

PayPal has strict rules governing the exchange of money so that no one person cheats another. If you decide not to adhere to these rules, you can be banned from ever using your account again. Among these rules are the obvious "taking payment for something you have not sent" and "failure to refund a contractually refundable item."

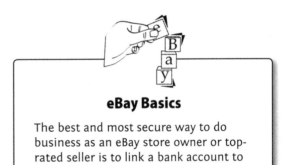

eBay Basics

The best and most secure way to do business as an eBay store owner or top-rated seller is to link a bank account to your PayPal account.

Now that you are all set, you have your eBay account set up, you have your PayPal account set up, your bank information is confirmed, and you are ready to go. It's time to find out what millions around the world are so hyped about and jump into eBay.

CHAPTER 4

Homeward Bound

In This Chapter

➤ Signing in again
➤ Navigation bar
➤ Search and ye shall find
➤ Categorically speaking

In this chapter you will be introduced to the main Home page of eBay. This is where every eBayer starts out when beginning or continuing the eBay adventure. To get to know this page is sort of like becoming familiar with the job description of a new job. You'll notice that eBay includes some links under more than one category, making it easier and more likely to find exactly what you're looking for.

You'll use many aspects of the Home page on a daily basis, and, as such, the Home page will be your first stop from now until the very end of your eBay journey (if that day ever comes, it has yet to come for me).

Home

So here we are, home at last. When you type in the web address www.ebay.com, you will come to the page that everyone comes to, the Home page. This is not a page you want to ignore. In fact, short of your My eBay page, this is the most important page there is. From this page, you can navigate everywhere on the website.

The top right corner, shown in figure 1, displays a series of links that can take you anywhere you want to go.

Figure 4.1

As you can see, the Home page gives you all the power of eBay on one page. Among the tools available to access this power are:

➤ Links to your My eBay page, the sell drop-down menu, community, and customer support.

➤ A search bar where you can enter the name of any item imaginable. The search engine offers an advanced feature, enhancing its usefulness.

➤ An All Categories menu, which can be found in two places on the Home page: on top of the page next to the search bar, and on the far left, where the categories are further delineated within the column. Click on either of the all categories arrow and you'll get a list of the major categories in a drop-down menu. This allows you to pinpoint your search for an item within a specified category rather than search all of eBay using just the search bar. The All Categories menu is especially helpful if you know off the top of your head exactly which category the item you seek is in.

➤ The rest of the page is particularly intriguing to frequent shoppers. Every day, eBay posts new and exciting deals, featured items, possible savings, and much, much more.

If you're an avid shopper, you will come to look at the eBay Home page once a day. By following this routine I have bought fantastic featured items and have taken advantage of particular deals that many others miss because they look at the page less frequently.

Sign In Again?

You may have noticed that signing into eBay is a daily requirement. You may find this slightly inconvenient, but studies have shown that e-commerce websites are often infiltrated by family, friends, and coworkers. And external infiltration by hackers is a constant threat. Being required to sign in every day is one way to keep these threats to a minimum.

eBay Expressions

URL is the initialism for Uniform Resource Locator, which refers to an Internet address.

You may want to check the Keep Me Signed In option so you aren't automatically signed out periodically throughout the day, which can be inconvenient, annoying, even aggravating. Again, if you share your computer or if others have access to your computer, you'll want to keep this box unchecked to thwart any misuse of your account.

When you type the URL www.eBay.com into the search engine, you will invariably have to sign in. Type in the user ID and password you created earlier. You can check the box asking if you want eBay to keep you signed in if you're not sharing your computer with anyone and other risks don't exist. After signing in, navigate to the Home page. You can do this easily by clicking the eBay logo on the top left of any eBay page.

Navigation Bar

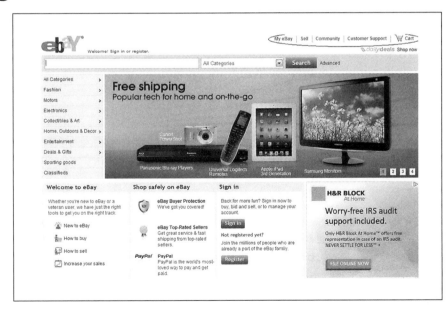

Figure 4.2

eBay Basics

You'll notice that many of eBay's important or most-used functions can be found on nearly every page.

Here we are finally. We are about to buy, sell, browse, and become full-fledged eBayers. Everything we need to begin is right here at our fingertips. Let's look at the navigation bar at the top right of the Home page in figure 4.2.

The navigation bar is available in nearly every page of eBay; proof positive that it is indeed an important part of eBay. There are four categories, and each category has a drop-down menu with multiple links. With these four categories and the corresponding links, you can navigate nearly anywhere on the entire site. It is a powerful toolbar and you should get to know it well. Let's take a more in-depth look at it.

My eBay

The first category is My eBay. Hover your mouse pointer over the My eBay category to see a drop-down menu (see figure 4.2) listing every link found on your My eBay page. Each link takes you to a different part of the My eBay page. Here is a list of the links in the My eBay menu:

➤ Summary

➤ Bids/offers

➤ Watch list

➤ Wish list

➤ All lists

➤ Purchase history

➤ Selling

➤ Saved searches

➤ Messages

Sell

The Sell category is essential to your success on eBay. This is where the party is. Becoming an eBay seller starts with the first link, Sell an Item. Hover your pointer over the Sell category to see the drop-down menu, which includes these links:

➤ Sell an item: This is the first step on the long path to becoming an eBay store owner and a top-rated seller. It will be the most-used link for all of you soon-to-be sellers.

➤ Check for instant offers: This is a relatively new and awesome tool for those who are selling their personal electronics. It's a fantastic tool in a day and age when next-generation electronics come on the market so quickly. This tool is perfect for those who want to purchase the newest and best electronic devices and are looking for ways to sell their last-generation device.

➤ Sell it for me: Just as it sounds, this link helps you find a store similar to a consignment shop through which you can sell your goods. This eBay trading assistant charges a fee for selling your items, but the rest of the proceeds from the sale goes to you.

➤ Seller information center: This is an area dedicated to assisting sellers with all types of information from making a listing and creating postage to using advanced tools and getting professional-level support.

Community

This category is essential if you wish to become a member of the vast eBay community. It is a digital version of going to a small business owners' meeting. It, too, has subcategories that are revealed in its drop-down menu, all of which will help you get involved in the eBay community:

➤ Announcements: This is where you can get information on what is currently going on in the eBay world, what's new, what changes have been made, and much more. It is rather important that serious eBayers make this one of the first pages they look at each day for much of the same reason a financier reads the *Wall Street Journal* daily.

➤ Answer center: What do you do after you sell an item? Is this item legally allowed to be listed on eBay? Whatever your question, the answer center is the place to go. You can find answers to most, if not all, of your eBay-related questions, or you can simply go to the FAQ section to get answers to themost commonly asked questions.

eBay Expressions

Most websites have an FAQ page for people to get answers to the most-asked questions. *FAQ* is the initialism for Frequently Asked Questions.

➤ Discussion forums: People in a digital community like to come together and discuss important topics related to that community, such as changes that should or should not be made, or just casually talk about life in that community. eBay is no different; it is a community and as such the people within that community have a voice and need a venue in which to be heard. This is that venue.

➤ Preview new features: If you want to know about and access the latest features on eBay, this is the place to go. eBay is constantly adding new features, and it would behoove all eBayers to be aware of them, especially those features that would help them grow their business.

➤ Green shopping: This is the place to be for the ecologically minded. Here you can shop for products that are safe for the environment. The page has numerous links to subcategories to simplify your search.

➤ Groups: Groups are created by eBay users and are open to everyone. Like any other group online, eBay groups have moderators, usage policies, and even a group charter.

➤ eBay top shared: When an item on eBay is so unique or unusual, people talk about it. Updated daily, this page gathers those items that have garnished the most attention, either through tweets, e-mails, or on Facebook.

Customer Support

When you have questions or run into trouble, which you are bound to do at some point during your eBay experience, the customer support link comes in handy. Besides offering basic help, this category has links that direct you to other forms of help:

➤ Customer support: This page is where you can find self-help assistance or opt to e-mail or call an actual customer service representative.

➤ Learning center: This link allows you to access the basics of eBay. You can teach yourself all there is to know about eBay in the learning center.

➤ Resolution center: eBay expects people who are doing transactions with each other to work out any problems that arise. Sometimes, though, that's not possible. When a dispute is at a standstill with no resolution in sight, eBay offers its resolution center to help solve the impasse.

➤ eBay university: eBay provides classes in an actual classroom setting taught by certified education specialists. While this book is designed to teach all you need to begin using eBay, there are many who prefer the structure of a classroom setting. Providing such a resource is further proof of how far eBay is willing to go to help every eBayer become an expert.

And the Links Keep Coming

The Home page has a plethora of features, links, and categories. At the bottom of the page is a box with columns of links much like the navigation bar except there are no drop-down menus, the links are right there. I will not ramble on about these links but simply point out the main categories and the links that go with them. Many are redundant and can be found on the navigation bar, many are self-explanatory, most will be elaborated on later in the book, and the rest you can click on and play around with. The following are the names of the columns followed by the links you will find under them:

➤ Buy: Registration, eBay buyer protection, bidding & buying help, stores, top products, brands on eBay

➤ Sell: Start selling, learn to sell, business sellers, affiliates

➤ eBay companies: eBay classifieds, shopping.com, half.com, PayPal, see all

➤ About eBay: Company info, investors, news, eBay ink blog, government relations, jobs, advertise with us, policies, contact us, tell us what you think

➤ Community: Announcements, answer center, discussion boards, preview new features, eBay giving works, eBay celebrity, groups, eBay top shared

➤ Gift center: eBay wish list, gift cards, gift guide, group gifts

➤ Tools: Downloads, developers, security center, eBay official time, site map

➤ eBay sites (This is where you tell eBay which country you live in.)

➤ Stay connected: Facebook, Twitter, eBay Mobile

Bottom Line

The Home page isn't the only page that offers resources. All pages on eBay have a line of links running along the bottom. Let's take a look.

About eBay

This link will take you to eBay's information pages. Everything you need to know about eBay can be found here such as stock information, earnings report, company news, and other such information that public companies must offer to the people that utilize or invest in the company.

Helpful Tip

Take some time to play around and explore the links on eBay. You'll be surprised by all the information eBay lays at your fingertips!

Here are the links you'll find running down the left side of the page:

➤ Who we are

➤ eBay connect

➤ Newsroom

➤ Social innovations

➤ Investors

➤ Careers

➤ Contact us

Security Center

This is a very important area. eBay goes to great lengths to ensure a safe and secure experience. It offers a lot of advice, as well as resources, on keeping your computer and your account safe. In the unlikely event of a security breach, eBay has a way for you to report it.

This page has tabs you can click on to access its various features:

➤ Protect your identity

➤ Protect your computer

➤ Report a problem

➤ More resources

Buyer Tools

This page offers desktop and mobile tools that enhance the buying experience on eBay. Let's face it, you can't continue to bid on that Ming vase if you walk away from your desktop, so eBay gives you ways to keep track of and continue bidding on an item.

Policies

You must be familiar with eBay's policies and procedures. As with any business, eBay has rules that need to be followed such as what you can and cannot list and eBay etiquette. This page also functions as the Help page with a plethora of links to help topics, as well as links to an eBay glossary, eBay acronyms, and an eBay A to Z list of help topics.

Stores

This is where you eventually want to end up listed as a seller: in the fabulous world of eBay stores. You can use this link to find stores that are selling what you want. This area also allows you to simply browse stores that are deemed popular and successful, and those that are highly recommended by eBayers and eBay itself.

eBay Wish List

This page is where you can sign up for, add items to, manage, and share your wish list. This is a new page and is bound to be one that is visited time and again.

Site Map

A site map can be found on most every website. It is pretty much a road map to every page on that website. eBay divides its site map into five categories:

1. Buy: Includes registration, categories, more ways to find items, and buying resources subcategories

2. Sell: Includes selling activities, selling resources, selling tools, and web stores subcategories

3. My eBay: Includes My Account and My Selling Account subcategories

4. Community: Includes Feedback, Connect, News, Marketplace Safety, And More Community Programs subcategories

5. Help: Includes Resources and Help Topics subcategories

eBay Official Time

This link provides you with the exact date and time anywhere in the United States and pinpoints the location of eBay headquarters.

Preview New Features

Do you want to see what's new and on the cutting edge of eBay buying and selling? This link will fill you in on all the latest features you can find on eBay.

Tell Us What You Think

Like most all companies, eBay would like to know what you think about your experience navigating and doing business on its site. This page gives you ample room to write your thoughts.

Search and Ye Shall Find

eBay offers a variety of ways for you to search for items. Prominently displayed on the Home page is a search bar in which you can type the name of the item you want. This is effective if you know exactly what you want. It can be used less specifically, too, if you know generally what you want. Just type in *shoes*, for instance, and a list of brand names will pop up from which you can narrow down your search.

You can opt to search all of eBay or get a little more specific by choosing a category to search in, say sporting goods.

The advanced search works in a similar way but offers a huge increase in specificity. For one thing, you can choose to type in more than one word or decide to exclude a word to get a more specific result. You can also look for an exact listing if you know the listing's item number. You can further narrow your search by specifying a price range. This helps greatly if you are dead set against going above a certain price.

Other choices to make your search more specific such as buying formats, shipping options, etc., can be checked off, and some of those check boxes are as follows:

➤ Auction

➤ Buy it Now

➤ Classified ads

➤ With PayPal accepted

➤ Listing ending times

There are enough check boxes to make your search so specific that you may have only one item to choose from.

Categorically Speaking

Another way of looking for what you want is by browsing the categories on the Home page. Although there might seem to be an endless supply of categories, eBay has done a fantastic job of limiting them to about three dozen.

Overall, your Home page is the second most important page in your eBay life. It will be the first page you see when you type in ebay.com and will be your best friend along with the My eBay page, which you will read about in the next chapter.

CHAPTER 5

My eBay

In this chapter you will be introduced to the very most important page in your eBay career, the My eBay page. This page is going to be the heart of your entire experience with eBay. Whether it's buying or selling one item or becoming an eBay entrepreneur, this page is going to be your control center. Every business has its headquarters, and this is yours on eBay. I cannot stress enough how important it is to learn every facet of this page.

My eBay

You have used your user name and password to log in for the very first time, now what? I recall when I logged in my first time, I went straight to an item I had had my eye on for days and made a bid. Eventually I was outbid, and I proceeded to sling several choice words at my monitor.

Better than jumping in feet first, you'd do well to make your first stop at your My eBay page, the most used and powerful tool at your disposal.

In your eBay career you will bid, buy, and sell. You will field e-mails, send feedback, print postage. All of this will be done from one place: your My eBay page. This is your control console. Everything you do, every sale you make, every message you get will be controlled from this page. Over the years, my eBay has gone through changes but it still remains an eBayer's central command center.

So let us take a look at this most important of all pages. You will notice some aspects of my eBay that are common to the home page such as the navigation bar, the bottom links, and the categories. But there is myriad more to see that you will become familiar with over time.

The Summary Page

eBay's default page when you click on my eBay is the Summary page. This page, of course, summarizes all your activities on eBay. On the left side of the screen, you'll see three tabs under My eBay: Summary. The first and most important is the Activity tab.

eBay Basics

Much like every other commerce site, eBay allows you to change how you view your My eBay page. One of your options is to change your landing page, which is the default page you land on when you go to a website or to your personal page on a website.

The page you first see when you choose to go to your My eBay page by default is the Summary page. To change the default page, look to the right opposite the Summary tabs and click on the Change link that follows "The My eBay landing page is set to Summary." Then choose the landing page you want from the drop-down menu and click Apply.

My Feedback

Contrary to popular belief, what people think about you does matter—at least on eBay. The first thing you will see when you look at the upper left of the page after My eBay: Summary is your user name and a number in parentheses. This number is the most important number you will have on eBay. It is your feedback score.

Your feedback score lets people know how you have conducted yourself on a sale or a purchase on eBay. Anyone can check out your feedback score and see what people have said about your business practices. The number itself doesn't say much. If you have a feedback score of 1,000 and 999 of those are negative, then you are not doing too well. However, if your score is 10 and all 10 are positive, then that is a 100 percent positive score; the percentage is the number that truly counts.

Several factors affect the type of feedback that people will leave for you. How fast did you ship an item you sold? How fast did you pay for an item purchased? What method of shipping did you use? There are even petty reasons, as there are in any business, for people to leave you bad as well as good feedback. For instance, there was a millimeter scratch in an item not visible in the posted photo, or the package was delivered an hour later than promised.

Always keep potential feedback in mind as you do business on eBay. Cater to each eBayer individually, because no two people will leave the same feedback for the same reason.

Feedback Profile

Once you click on a feedback score, you are taken directly to that person's feedback profile. This is where you can read about how that person conducts business. The following is what you will find:

➤ How much feedback this person has

➤ The percentage of positive versus negative feedback this person has

➤ How many positive, neutral, and negative ratings this person has received in the last one, six, and twelve months

➤ How long this person has been a member

➤ Feedback left for you as a seller and as a buyer, and all the feedback you've left for others

You may want to pay attention to a few other points of interest on this page. For example, there is a box labeled Detailed Seller Ratings that allows a person leaving feedback to rate this person's strengths and weaknesses on a scale of 1 to 5. Was their communication timely? Was the item different from the description of the item you received? Was a quickly shipped item deserving of a high rating? It is not a comprehensive rating, but it is a great glimpse into an eBayer's strengths?

Another little feature that is worth taking a look at is the member quick links. Here you can click on any of the following links:

➤ View items for sale

➤ View ID history

➤ Add to favorite sellers

➤ View eBay my world

➤ View reviews and guides

Helpful Tip

When checking out someone's feedback ratings, most people are going to look at just the percentage rating. But it never hurts to access all the information about an eBayer that's available. Even if the person has less than a 1 percent negative feedback rating, it may pay to see exactly what went wrong during those sour transactions so you're prepared if the same thing happens to you.

The Activity Tab

The Activity tab breaks down the various ways you have to keep track of all your buying and selling activities.

Figure 5.1

There are three categories within the activity that are further broken down into subcategories:

Buy

This section keeps track of the bids and offers you've made, those that you didn't win, and those you deleted. The more transactions you're involved in, the more helpful this activity summary will be to you.

Lists

You can keep track of all your lists at once, just your watch list, just your wish list, or even create a new list in this section. If you're looking for an item to buy but you want to wait to see where the bidding price is going, you can put the listing on your watch list. You're allowed to select up to two hundred items to watch. If you want an item, but you're not sure you're ready to buy it, you can put it on your wish list. You can even share your wish list on Facebook.

eBay Basics

The watch list helps you keep track of the number of bids you've made, the amount of each bid, the current bid on the item, and alerts you to when the listing is closing. This is a window shopper's dream, sitting in front of your laptop and choosing a boatload of items to look at without leaving the house.

Sell

This section helps you keep track of everything you're selling. It's further broken in subcategories, including all selling, scheduled, active, sold, unsold, shipping labels, deleted.

Additional Features

Continuing down the left side of the page, you'll find buying reminders, announcements, and shortcuts. The shortcuts will quickly take you to various other categories such as my vehicles, buyer tools, eBay mobile apps, and more. You can edit these shortcut categories to include those that you will use most frequently by clicking on the edit shortcuts button at the bottom of the list.

The Messages Tab

Click on the Messages tab and your eBay e-mail page will open. This is the method by which all eBay communication is handled. Here you can pick up messages from buyers who have questions about an item you're selling, sellers with answers to questions you've asked about their item, and read announcements from eBay.

Constant contact during buying and selling on eBay is as important as a salesperson making a follow-up call to close a deal.

eBay Basics

Communication is important when doing business on eBay. It's likely you'll send and receive many messages during your time with eBay. It is up to you and the person you're doing business with to be in sync. You can learn more about the importance of communication at eBay's learning center.

Good communication is important during disputes as well. eBay mediates disputes, but it's up to you to supply documentation that supports your position. Part of that documentation is having copies of the e-mails that went back and forth between you and the person you're having the dispute with.

The Account Tab

Here is all your account information in one place, from personal information to site preferences to resolution center. It even includes information about your PayPal account.

Helpful Tip

I can't stress this enough: change your password on a regular basis. Although eBay has incredible security, the weak link any transaction you make on eBay is you. Your own PC is vulnerable to viruses and people hacking you, someone could look over your shoulder as you input your password, and so on. So as a general rule, change your password on a monthly basis if possible.

Hover your mouse over the Account Summary tab, and you'll see a list of links that will direct you to different aspects of your account. Many of these links can also be found on the left of your screen under My Account in the My eBay Views box. These links allow you to customize your account, offer resources, and help you keep track of all your selling activities.

The Account Summary

This page informs you of all your recent activities, apprises you of your latest invoice to be paid, fees, credits, payments, and refunds. This is the control center for all your personal financial information, personal eBay preferences, and all information that you can possibly store, change, or customize.

The page is divided into three categories—Account Summary, Payment Method for Seller Fees, and Your PayPal Account Information.

It's important to keep your information updated, financial accounts linked perfectly, communication and alerts set efficiently, and so on, so everything is in order and easy to access at any moment. Here is a rundown of the links:

➤ Personal information: This page is divided into three sections—Account Information, E-Mail and Contact Information, and Financial Information. Each section is further divided into categories that you can edit to reflect your personal information.

You can review and change your user name, passwords, telephone numbers, e-mail, secret question for password retrieval, and Instant Message if you choose to use it. You can update your checking account, credit card, PayPal account, and payment method. I hope I don't need to repeat that this information should be guarded with your life.

➤ Addresses: Here you will find your registration, or main contact, address, and the ship-to and ship-from addresses. Although you, as a beginner, may find this a little pointless, the bigger eBay stores that may have different warehouses that they ship from, for instance, make good use of this information.

➤ Communication preferences: This page is divided into five sections—Delivery Options, Member Communications, Buyer, General Preferences, and Promotions and Surveys. You can personalize each section to suit you and your business.

➤ Site preferences: If you want to change your eBay selling or payment settings, this is the page to go to. You can also block specific eBayers from bidding or buying from your store, or specify shipping options.

➤ Manage communication with buyers: eBay offers to send generic e-mails automatically when a buyer wins an auction, checks out, is late with a payment; to update an order with shipping information; and to remind a buyer to leave feedback.

➤ Seller dashboard: This page gives you a rundown of your sales to date.

➤ Feedback: Displays items awaiting feedback and the recent feedback you've received.

➤ Seller account: This is the same as your account summary page.

Helpful Tip

One of the main causes of negative feedback is bad communication. Believe it or not, some people will demand their money back if you are simply a day late responding to an inquiry. Always, always, always e-mail, respond and send courtesy or thank-you notes. It is a great way to be remembered and get repeat business; not doing so is a great way to get negative

➤ Donation account: This page gives you the opportunity to contribute to charities.

➤ Resolution center: The eBay Resolution Center provides a venue for eBay to mediate any problems two eBayers may have when doing business together.

➤ PayPal Account: You can access your PayPal account from this page to review your account history and profile.

➤ Marketing tools: On this page, eBay introduces you to various tools to help you as a seller.

➤ Subscriptions: This page offers various resources that help you as an eBayer that you can subscribe to.

The Applications Tab

Applications is the newest feature on My eBay and as of the writing of this book, it is available in Beta form. It is divided into two sections—Your Apps and Featured Apps. There is also an Apps Center link on the top right side of the page that will take you to a page with all the apps available through eBay.

eBay Expressions

App is an abbreviation for *application*. An application is a small program with a specialized function created for end users, people like you. Some are fun (games, e-readers), some are helpful (GPS, weather reports), and some are extremely useful for getting complex or tedious tasks done quickly (postage, metric conversions).

My eBay apps help your eBay business be more efficient and can even reduce your costs and otherwise enhance your business.

A UPS app, for instance, may save a lot of time and money by streamlining shipping. Take a look at the available apps and see how efficient your business can become.

Overall, I cannot think of a more important page than the My eBay page. It is your command center. It is where you can control, manage, change, and customize every single aspect of eBay. It is where you keep an eye on every single transaction.

eBay painstakingly created this page to ensure keeping track of your eBay transactions wouldn't become overwhelming. I cannot think of another page that eBay has created since its inception that makes the lives of every one of the millions of eBayers easier.

PART TWO

Buying and Selling

CHAPTER 6

Exploring and Searching on eBay

In This Chapter

➤ The tradition of trading

➤ Window shopping from home

➤ Browsing versus searching

➤ Results of your search

Many eBay sellers cut their teeth on eBay by browsing and searching. In this chapter, you will learn all the basics of exploring eBay and searching for just the right item.

Before There Was eBay

Have you ever gone to a yard sale and found something for such a low price you had to buy it even though it had no significant, intrinsic, or sentimental value to you—it just caught your eye? It was inexpensive and you went out that day to shop—so you bought it. Will you ever use it or even display it? Perhaps not.

Trading, whether with money or with other items, is a tradition that has existed nearly since the beginning of humanity. Only in modern times has it become a matter of luxury as well as necessity. eBay is the very incarnation of that idea. It is the amalgamation of trade, yard sales, garage sales, fire sales, and pawn shops all rolled into an enterprise with principles, values, rules, and regulations.

From Soup to Nuts

Many people spend a lot of time exploring eBay before making their first purchase. Some may feel overwhelmed by the extent of what eBay has to offer; others find the variety of purchasing possibilities exciting. Whether you're just testing the waters by taking a gander at what eBay has to offer or you're ready to plunge into the whole eBay experience, learning the art of searching on eBay is a must.

If you feel a little intimidated in the beginning, don't worry; most people find the eBay experience addicting and it probably won't take long for you to get reeled into the whole online shopping experience. The excitement of an auction and the uncertainty of whether you'll win the item you're bidding on can be as addicting as gambling.

Helpful Tip

When you begin bidding on an item, it's best to have an idea of how much you're willing to spend on it. Many times people get so wrapped up in the bidding process that they end up winning the auction item at a price above what they can afford.

The sheer volume and variety of listings can keep people glued to their computer screens for hours. You might find that antique dresser your grandmother had, a favorite toy you lost and never thought you'd find again, or that hard-to-find car part for the 1959 Edsel you're rebuilding.

eBay Expressions

Buy It Now is an option eBay offers that allows you to buy an item without going through the bidding process. Some auctions give buyers a choice of bidding or out and out buying the item; some auctions offer only one or the other.

Many items on eBay are being sold at a better price than you would find at most brick-and-mortar retail stores. Right this moment, there is a laptop that would sell for $499 retail in your local electronics shop, and I see it on eBay for a Buy It Now price of $199.

If you were to ask, "What can I find on eBay," I could only answer with a question, "What can't you find on eBay?" I'm referring to the UFO photos, 100-year-old lost witches' spells, and a jewelry store that make up just a tiny fraction of what I saw on one afternoon. Really, if it exists, you'll likely find it on eBay. And that is what makes eBay so special, so unique, so incredible. It represents opportunity; it is the digitized version of America's slogan Land of Opportunity.

Window Shopping from Your Home

When we go window shopping from store to store, we're just checking out what's available and at what prices. We're not really shopping for anything in particular. You can do this on eBay without leaving home, even without creating an eBay account. And on eBay, you can look at thousands of items in a few hours as opposed to the few dozen items you can see while window shopping in one weekend.

eBay Basics

Shopping on eBay saves time (you can shop for hundreds of items a day) and energy (you're not using gas to power a vehicle to drive you around town searching for that just-right item). You may want to spend some of your extra time in a gym to make up for all the extra sitting you'll be doing shopping and selling on eBay.

Online retail websites spend a lot of time and money to provide consumers with the tools they need to make good buying decisions. High-resolution pictures and a way to interact with the item are just two of these tools. They detail the item in laypeople's terms and some sellers give the pros and cons of their models as compared to other manufacturers' models.

So in my opinion, nothing beats window shopping online. And eBay is the granddaddy of window shopping, giving shoppers the opportunity to choose among hundreds of sellers to get just the right item at just the right price.

eBay Basics

A huge number of eBay purchases come from impulse buys stemming from in-home Internet window shopping.

Window Shopping on eBay

Every single item on eBay has its own page, often with a detailed description of that item. You can find many different sellers of one particular item, and each seller's page will have its own flair and its own sales pitch. You can window shop these pages for fun or to find a particular item in the exact condition, the exact color, or the exact size you want.

You can surf page after page, looking through featured items, whole categories, or comparing one seller's items to another. While you are surfing, every single item, whether you click on it or not, has its price tag in full view. It is actually part of the brief description in the list of items that pop up as a result of clicking a category or using the Search feature.

If you want to know more about the item, you simply click on the item's name or picture and a page called a posting pops up. The seller has created this posting to provide an attention-grabbing sales pitch of that item. More often than not, it's the sales pitch that draws interest to the item and determines how high the bidding will go. The sales pitch is one of the most, perhaps the most, important part of the page.

Browsing

When you go on eBay to shop, you will notice two ways to find an item: by browsing or by searching.

Browsing is best compared to window shopping. You begin with a broad sense of what you're looking for and browse through eBay's well-structured category system.

Let's say you want a video game, but you do not have any particular game in mind—you just want one you have never played. Here's what you do:

➤ Go to the left side of your Home page

➤ Hover your cursor over All Categories, Electronics, or Entertainment

➤ Click on Video Games

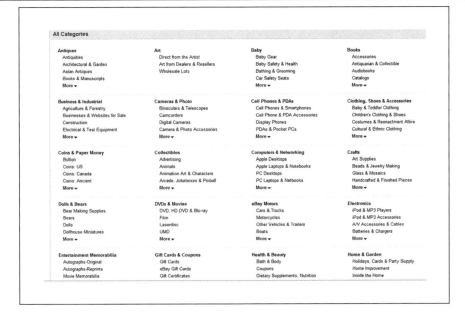

Figure 6.1

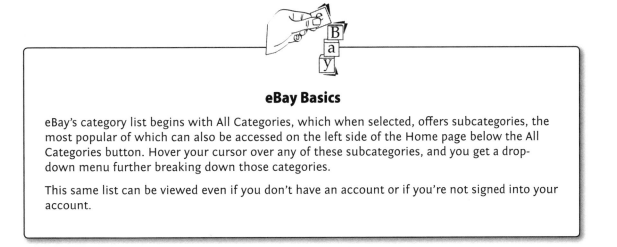

eBay Basics

eBay's category list begins with All Categories, which when selected, offers subcategories, the most popular of which can also be accessed on the left side of the Home page below the All Categories button. Hover your cursor over any of these subcategories, and you get a drop-down menu further breaking down those categories.

This same list can be viewed even if you don't have an account or if you're not signed into your account.

After you click the subcategory Video Games, you are routed to a page titled Video Games & Systems, where you will find even more subcategories. Click Games on the left side of the page, and you're routed to a page that lists games. You will probably get tens if not hundreds of thousands of listings. This is where the next parts of browsing comes in.

Refining

On the left side of the page is a list of popular products. If you see anything that interests you on that list, click on it. Otherwise, look toward the top of the page, where you will find four tabs:

➤ All items

➤ Auctions only

➤ Buy It now

➤ Products & Reviews (now in Beta)

If you don't care whether you browse items that are offered only through auction or only as Buy it Now, click on All Items. The category section on the left side of the page gives you options to hone into the type of video game that might interest you. The options are:

➤ Platform: The system on which the game can be played, for example, Xbox, Nintendo Wii, PlayStation

➤ Genre: The category of game, for example, action/adventure, role playing, simulation

➤ Condition: the condition and age of the game

➤ Price: You can specify a price range you're willing to pay

➤ Rating: Includes EC (early childhood), T (teen), M (mature)

➤ Buying formats: Again, you can choose auctions only or Buy It Now only, among other options

➤ Show only: You can choose to see only those items that have free shipping or that can be returned, for example

➤ Location: The geographical location of the item, North America or US only, for example

➤ Distance: How far the item is from your location, for those times you want to pick up the item instead of having it shipped to you.

Of course, this is an example of just one category, but you get the idea of the range of options eBay gives you to refine your browsing categories and help you pinpoint the exact item you're looking for.

Once you have made the proper refinements, you will get listings based solely on those parameters. There will be much fewer items to browse through, and your choices will be very close to, if not exactly, what you're looking for.

The Search Bar

You might wonder why you would use the Search bar now rather than when you were on the Home page. The answer is simple.

Let's say you don't know the exact name of what you want, for example you forgot the name Guitar Hero World Tour and only remember *Guitar*. If you typed the word *Guitar* in the Home page Search bar, you would come up with hundreds of thousands of listings in many different categories, most of which have nothing to do with video games.

Helpful Tip

One trick some people use when searching for an item is to type a common misspelling of the item in the search box.

If you type *Guitar* in the Search bar on the Video Games & Systems page, you get only the names of video games with the word *guitar* in it, and you'll find your game right away.

The Search bar is used in the same manner whether you're browsing or searching.

Advanced Search

This feature offers so many ways to narrow your search that you might end up with very few hits. Being too specific may exclude some items that you would be interested in considering, and you may not get the best deal because there won't be enough results for you to be able to compare prices or sellers.

Look through your options on the Advanced Search page and explore all their subcategories. Play around with changing the parameters for a particular search to see how it affects your results. Here are the major parameters you can choose within Advanced Search.

➤ Enter keywords or item number: You also get the option of search for some of the words, all of the words, words in any order, and more from a drop-down menu.

➤ In this category: choose the category from the All Categories drop-down menu.

➤ Search including: You have two choices here: Title and Description or Completed Listing

➤ Price: You can enter the price range you're willing to consider

➤ Buying formats: You have three choices here: Auction, Buy It Now, or Classified ads

➤ Show results: You can choose shipping options, sales items, and more.

➤ Location: Do you want to consider items from the United States only or items that are close enough for you to pick up? Here you can specify the item's location.

➤ Currency: You have a drop-down menu from which to choose the country's currency you'd like make your transaction with.

➤ Sellers: This is where you can specify if you want to do business only with those who have an eBay store or who are on your Saved Sellers list, and more.

Searching

To start us off, we will be creating a results page using the Search feature. In this case, the keywords we will use are *lockback knife* since I will be using this as an example throughout this buying section. So you enter the keywords *lockback knife* and you're on to the next step.

Helpful Tip

eBay's Search bar is not case sensitive, so you don't need to worry about capitalization.

You will be using the Search feature the most if you're not window shopping. As you can see in figure 6.1, you can be as specific as entering the model name, *falcon IV lockback knives* or as vague as entering *knife.*

Possible categories within which the item may be listed can be found on the left side of each results page. In our example, the two categories with the most listings that match our search are Collectibles and Sporting Goods. You can click on one of these categories, which then leads to another offer of possible subcategories. With each choice you narrow down the possibilities until you are left with a reasonable number of items to search through, hopefully finding the exact knife you are looking for.

The Search feature is no different from any other Search feature. However, eBay makes it more intricate and at the same time easier to use, especially with the Advanced Search feature, which was discussed above. eBay tries to make sure you find the item you want to find without having to look through every single one of the millions of listings.

Results of Your Search

So here we are, faced with the listings that resulted from the lockback knife search. The results could fill up one page or a multitude of pages, but each is structured the same way.

Related Searches

Aside from the links, Navigation bars, and such that are common to most every eBay page, the results pages offer another useful tool. Below the Search bar is a list of related searches. This feature lists several keywords similar to those you used in your search.

In my search for a lockback knife, for example, eBay listed *folding knife* and *pocketknife*, among others, as related searches that may yield more successful results.

Categorizing Your Search

The left side of the page contains a column with options that help you narrow down your search. These options are the same ones used in the Advanced Search page.

Based on what you know about the item, you want to click on the category in which it is most likely to be found. Sticking with the knife example, the category Knives, Swords & Blades seems to be our best bet. After clicking on that category, our options are further narrowed. Our example is a type of folding knife, so we click on Folding Knives.

You're directed to another page where you can specify modern or vintage or further narrow down your search by clicking on a particular brand name.

Helpful Tip

Keep in mind that eBay does not allow certain items to be listed. Knives are allowed only if they meet specific criteria. The lockback knife not only fits the criteria, but is offered on eBay in abundance.

When you click on a brand name—let's say we choose Smith & Wesson—you are directed to another page that lists just Smith & Wesson folding knives and allows you to further narrow down your search.

The features become more and more specialized as you work your way to specificity. Each page offers more subcategories to the subcategories, so you can continue to narrow down your search using the new options that are available to you.

Auction or Buy It Now

eBay is known first and foremost as an auction site. But not all listings on eBay are auctions. Look above the first listing on a results page. You'll see four tabs, each representing a

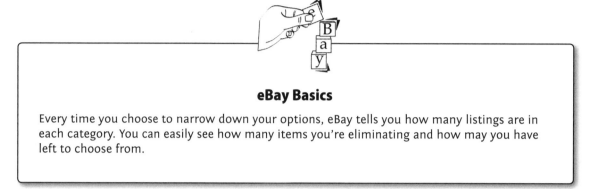

eBay Basics

Every time you choose to narrow down your options, eBay tells you how many listings are in each category. You can easily see how many items you're eliminating and how may you have left to choose from.

different way a listing can be handled:

➤ All items: This is the default tab, with every type of listing, no matter how it's being sold.

➤ Auction only: Here listings are sold by auction. They may or may not have a reserve price, but these are true auctions.

➤ Buy it now: This option shows listings that have a fixed priced. This option is useful if you're in a hurry for an item or you just don't want to bother with an auction.

➤ Products and reviews: Currently in Beta testing phase, this features items that have been reviewed by fellow eBayers, a feature very common to e-commerce sites.

Changing Your View

Search results are typically laid out in order of best match. As with nearly everything else on eBay, you can change the way these results are sorted and viewed.

Right under the tabs to the left is a View As option, which allows you to see your results in list (the default) or gallery format, or side-by-side in which the traditional auctions are on one side and the Buy It Now items are on the other side.

The order in which results are sorted can be changed using the Sort By drop-down menu under the tabs to the right. Best Match is the default, but your results can be ordered by time, price, or location.

The Listings

Now that you've honed in your search, the fun part begins: looking at the listings. All sellers include a listing title, price (which always reflects the current high bid), and picture. eBay provides the number of bids for the listing, the price, and the amount of time the auction has left.

Helpful Tip

When entering your keywords in the Search bar, try misspelling them. Some great opportunities are missed because sellers aren't great spellers.

While many people begin a search with price in mind, some listings will have pictures or descriptions that jump at you. Others will have titles that capture your imagination or speak to you. There are strategies to buying but for the time being, browse around, see what you like, get a feel for things and soon you will be in and out with the item you want in the time it took to read the first paragraph of this chapter.

CHAPTER 7

Bidding Considerations

In This Chapter

➤ The results page: what to consider

➤ The importance of feedback

➤ Types of non-auctions

In this chapter we will go over what needs to be considered before deciding to bid on an item. You'll get a tour of the results page, which will arm you with information that will help you make smart decisions when it's time to bid. You will learn about feedback and how that can help you be a better eBayer, and you'll get introduced to the different types of non-auctions that eBay offers.

The Results Page Listings

Each listing on the results page includes information about the item. A picture of the item is on the left, followed by the item description, return policy, special shipping options, and a tool to enlarge the photo.

A top-rated seller badge is next in line if the seller of the item has that classification. As one would think, top-rated sellers provide their customers with a buying experience of the highest quality. You can hardly go wrong doing business with a seller donning a top-rated seller badge.

Helpful Tip

Frequently on eBay, you'll find more than one listing offered by different sellers that match all your criteria. With all else being equal, compare the sellers' feedback and choose the one with the highest accolades.

Move farther to the right and you'll have the column that specifies the buying options—Bids (with the number of bids specified), Buy It Now, and/or Best Offer.

To the right of the buying options is the amount the item is being listed for or the amount the bidding has reached. The bidding amount is updated in real time. You may have to refresh your page to see the most current information.

The listings on the results page concludes with the days, hours, and minutes left in the auction. Keep in mind that bidding continues until the auction ends. But using the Buy It Now option or having your Best Offer accepted will end the auction.

The Listing Page

You've combed through your listing results and are interested in taking a closer look at a few of the listings. The next step is to click on the photo or the item description to get more detailed information about it.

Item Description and Bidding Information

At the top center of the item's listing page is the Item Condition information, which tells you whether the item is new, used, refurbished, with tags, in working order, and so on. For a full list of item categories and what they mean, you can go to http://pages.ebay.com/help/sell/item-condition.html. Underneath Item Condition is Time Left information, which gives you the number of days, hours, minutes, and even seconds left in the auction.

A highlighted box with all the transaction information is further down. To the left is the current bid, followed by how many bids have been made up to this point.

Helpful Tip

Click on the number of bids and you'll find a list of the bidders. Click on a bidder, and you get his or her bidding history. Any knowledge you glean from examining the bidders' history may give you a leg up during the bidding process.

Below the current bid is a box for you to fill in your bid amount. eBay tells you the minimum bid you can make right below the box. Once you place your bid, you click on the big, blue Place Bid button.

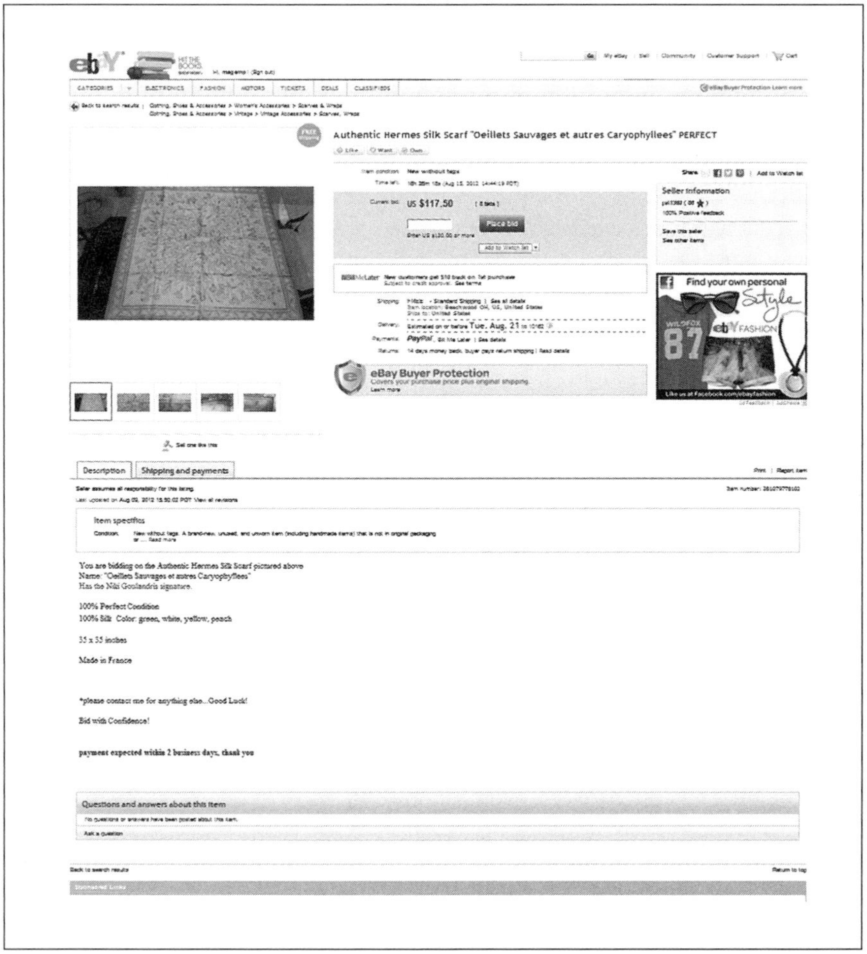

Figure 7.1

If you're not ready to place a bid, you can add the item to your watch list, wish list, or any other list you've created.

Checking Out Seller Information

As part of your research into each listing, you'll want to take a look at the Seller Information to the right of the Place Bid button.

First is the member ID, which is the name the seller goes by on eBay. Following is the seller feedback score in parentheses. This score is calculated from the number of positive, neutral, and negative scores received by the seller.

➤ Positive: +1

➤ Neutral: 0

➤ Negative: -1

Next to the feedback score is a colored star. The score determines the star's color, and each color represents the score level. You need a score of at least 10 to earn a yellow star. When your score hits 50, you've earned a blue star. Here are the levels:

➤ Yellow star: 10–49 points

➤ Blue star: 50–99 points

➤ Turquoise star: 100– 499 points

➤ Purple star: 500–999 points

➤ Red star: 1,000–4,999 points

➤ Green star: 5,000–9,999 points

➤ Yellow shooting star: 10,000–24,999 points

➤ Turquoise shooting star: 25,000–49,000 points

➤ Purple shooting star: 50,000–99,999 points

➤ Red shooting star: 100,000–499,999 points

➤ Green shooting star: 500,000–999,999 points

➤ Silver shooting star: 1,000,000 points or more

The information below the seller ID and rating is the percentage of positive feedback the seller has earned.

Shipping and Payment

Below the highlighted bidding box are the shipping details:

➤ Shipping: Includes fee, type of shipping, location of the item, and where the seller will ship (United States, worldwide, and so on).

➤ Delivery: Estimated range of delivery, including the seller's handling time. This time depends on shipping speed selected and confirmation that your payment has cleared.

➤ Payments: Includes PayPal, of course, Bill Me Later, and See Details link that will take you to the section of the page describing all the payment methods this seller accepts.

eBay Expressions

The Bill Me Later payment option is just like it sounds: you pay for the item with a credit card, but you're not billed right away. Most, but not all, items are eligible of this option. If the item you're interested in is eligible, the Bill Me Later option will be available. Click on that link and follow the directions.

➤ Returns: A brief description of the seller's return policy. Click on the Read Details link and you'll be directed to the section of the page that goes into the policy in more detail.

Be sure you read this section carefully so there aren't any surprises down the road. Don't overlook the shipping and handling costs, if any, and be sure to add these fees to the item's final cost before you decide to bid on the item. The shipping fees can put you over the maximum amount you're willing to pay for the item.

Below the shipping details is a link to the eBay Buyer Protection Plan. Click on this link and you can read all about how to handle any issues that may arise between you and a seller.

A little farther down the page is a gavel icon next to the Sell One Like This link. If you're a seller and have a similar item you'd like to sell, click on this link and eBay will automatically fill in some of the information required for the listing. Be sure to look this over carefully.

Continuing down the page, you'll find the section that details the item description and more detailed information on shipping and payment terms. Both sections should be read over carefully.

Pay particular attention to how the item is described. You may be looking for a pristine antique, but deep into the item's description is a list of dents, nicks, or missing pieces. If you don't read through the description and then win the item, you'll be disappointed by your purchase. You'll probably feel you paid too much for it since you were bidding on what you believed to be a flawless piece. You can't return an item or back out of a deal because you misread the description.

At the bottom of the listing is a place where you can ask a question of the seller. Don't hesitate to ask questions about the item. The more you know, the better bidder you'll be.

Non-Auction Buying Options

As we've already seen, the auction isn't the only way to buy on eBay. You also have the Best Offer and Buy It Now options.

Best Offer

If you have a specific price in mind for the item you want to buy and a seller lists the Best Offer option as one of the acceptable buying avenues, then you can follow the process to make the seller an offer. The seller has a choice of accepting or rejecting your offer, or making a counteroffer.

Here are the steps to take to submit your offer to a seller who accepts best offers:

1. Sign in

2. Go to the listing page

3. Click on Make Offer on the listing page

4. Enter the amount of your offer

5. Add a message to the seller (optional) in the appropriate box

6. Click on Review Offer

7. Review your offer and click on Submit Offer.

Now you wait for the seller's response to your offer.

Buy It Now

Some people just don't like to be bothered with the bidding process. If you're one of those people, Buy It Now is a great option.

eBay Basics

Some listings offer both the Buy It Now and the auction options. In most cases, the Buy It Now option disappears once bidding begins.

Once you have your listing results, go to the column on the left of the page and scroll down until you see the Buying Formats category. Click Buy It Now, and all your listing results will be only those that offer this option.

If you've factored in shipping costs and are willing to buy the item at the Buy It Now price, then click the Buy It Now button. Then click the Commit to Buy and Pay Now buttons when you're directed to them.

You can click the Add to Cart button if you don't want to buy the item right away.

The Shopping Cart

Adding an item to your shopping cart has advantages and disadvantages. First you need to know that putting an item in your shopping cart doesn't reserve it for you. It's still out there available to anyone who wants it. The exceptions are if you've committed to buy the item by winning an auction, having a Best Offer accepted, or clicking on Buy It Now.

Some of the advantages are that you have a choice of paying sellers separately or all together, if they all accept the same payment method. You're also not committed to buy the item, unless, of course, you won it at auction, or bought it through Buy It Now or Best Offer. You can have items in your cart that you want to compare to each other or keep track of so you can see how much you're spending.

CHAPTER 8

The Auction

In This Chapter

➤ How to value on an item
➤ Bidding rules
➤ Bidding strategies
➤ Types of auctions

In this chapter you will learn how to put a value on an item so you don't overbid. You will learn about the different types of auctions that eBay offers and learn about some of eBay's rules and services that will help you navigate strategically through the bidding process. After reading this chapter, you will be able to stand up to those more experienced than you and deal with their shenanigans. Let's get started!

Before Determining Your Bid

Okay. So you want to take advantage of the potential deals and assured excitement an auction has to offer. You've browsed and searched and compared prices and have finally found exactly what you're looking for. You've reviewed the item description and shipping policy, and you've checked out the seller's ratings. There is one more step you need to take to ensure you get the right item at the right price.

Determine Market Value

Before you set off bidding blindly on an item, you want to have a sense of how much the market deems this item to be worth. So do your research. You definitely don't want to pay too much for it. After all, isn't that one of the reasons you're shopping on eBay? Here are some ways to do your research:

> ➤ Selling price: Check the selling price of similar items on eBay. Be sure you take into account shipping costs and condition of each item.

> ➤ Brick-and-mortar stores: Check the major brick-and-mortar stores that carry this item. What are they charging for it? Shopping at a conventional store may not be as much fun as bidding on eBay, but if you can find what you want at a cheaper price somewhere else, buy it there!

> ➤ The Internet: Search the Internet for the item. You may find the deal you're looking for at one of the many discount shopping websites.

Depending on the type of person you are, bidding can be exciting or stressful or both. To alleviate the stress, or bring you down to earth so you don't make rash decisions, you need to go into the bidding process armed with information. Knowing the market value of the item you want to buy will help you set a maximum price for it. If you win the item, you'll be confident that you didn't pay too much for it; lose the item, and you won't be too disappointed because you'll know you didn't overpay.

Bidding Rules

Before you start placing bids, become familiar with eBay's rules and User Agreement. They exist to make the whole eBay experience safe and fair for everyone. The rules are basic and straightforward; if you use your common sense, you're likely to end up following eBay's rules naturally. But before you plunge into bidding, it's a good idea to understand eBay's bidding parameters. Here are some rules you must follow:

> ➤ Once you place a bid, you've made a commitment to buy that item. In fact, you've entered into a binding contract.

> ➤ You are under obligation to pay for the item you bought or won.

> ➤ Your contact information must be correct. Buyers and sellers need to be able to communicate with each other.

> ➤ You must want the item you're bidding on. You can't bid on your own item or on an item being sold by a friend or relative just to create a bidding frenzy.

> ➤ Under certain very limited circumstances, you are allowed to cancel or withdraw your bid. For instance, if you withdraw your bid because of a bidding error when the item has over 12 hours of bidding time left, you're required to enter another bid. For more information, go to ebay.com/help/buy/bid-retract.html.

> ➤ You are not allowed to circumvent eBay and try to buy an item directly from the seller.

eBay Expressions

When anyone bids on an item with the intent to increase its price, soup up the bidding process, or otherwise enhance the listing, that person is guilty of shill bidding. This includes a seller who bids on his or her own item. Shill bidding is against eBay's rules and even against the law in some places.

Bidding Strategies

You know what you want to bid on, you know the rules, now you're ready to jump into the eBay bidding fray. You're looking at the listing and see that your desired item has already received six bids from four different bidders. Is there any hope of winning the bid when you're bidding against a number of more experienced bidders? Should you just give up? Absolutely not! You just need to understand the bidding process and get acquainted with the bidding strategies that are available to you.

Helpful Tip

Most bidding strategies look down on bidding early in an auction. But some eBayers make an early bid to get daily status reports on that item. Another way to keep track of auctions is to put them on your Watch List.

Bidding by Increments

The seller sets the starting price of an item. Once the first bid is placed, eBay dictates the minimum amount required for each additional bid. This minimum amount is determined by the amount of the previous bid, which is, of course, the current high bid. Here is the formula eBay uses:

Bidding Increments Table

Current Price	Bid Increment
1¢–99¢	5¢
$1.00–$4.99	25¢
$5.00–$24.99	50¢
$25.00–$99.99	$1.00
$100.00–$249.99	$2.50
$250.00–$499.99	$5.00
$500.00–$999.99	$10.00
$1,000.00–$2,499.99	$25.00
$2,500.00–$4,999.99	$50.00
$5,000.00 and up	$100.00

So if Bidder A places a $2.50 bid on an item, Bidder B would need to bid at least $2.75, 25¢ more than the previous bid.

Auctions last for a number of days. Does that mean you have to stay glued to your computer, finger poised, waiting to make that next bid? Of course not; who would want to or be able to do that? So eBay has instituted proxy bidding for standard auctions.

eBay Expressions

A proxy is a person or entity that has the authority and power to act for another.

Proxy Bidding

One of the reasons eBay has become so popular is that it has implemented a lot of work-arounds.

One popular bidding strategy is to cut to the chase and bid the most you'll pay for the item (remembering to take any shipping or other additional costs into consideration). So if the seller sets the starting bid at $20 and you're willing to pay up to $250, you bid $250.

Helpful Tip

There is nothing more frustrating than losing an auction by mere pennies. One strategy to avoid this is to make your maximum bid an unpredictable number. If the maximum you're willing to pay for the item is $50.00, bid something like $50.76. If the second to the last bid of the auction is $50.75, you've won by a penny!

Are you wondering how you can get a great deal on an item if you show your hand at the very beginning of the auction? Well, you're really not showing your hand because eBay keeps your maximum bid hidden from everyone else (and everyone else's maximum bid hidden from you). So now eBay's proxy bidding comes into play.

Once you place a maximum bid, no matter if it's $5 or $5,000 more than the current high bid, eBay automatically places your bid at the current high price plus the minimum incremental amount required by the predetermined formula put forth in the bidding increments table. Referring to eBay's formula, and assuming there are two bidders with you being Bidder B, this is how the incremental bidding for the first six bids would play out even after you've placed your $250 maximum:

> ➤ Bidder A: $20.00
> ➤ Bidder B: $20.50
> ➤ Bidder A: $21.00
> ➤ Bidder B: $21.50
> ➤ Bidder A: $22.00
> ➤ Bidder B: $22.50

eBay Basics

When placing a bid, don't forget to hit that Confirm button. Some people in their excitement think they have placed their bid but are left in the dust because they didn't take that next step to confirm their bid.

By proxy, eBay's computers act on your behalf and automatically place your bids at the lowest bid necessary, which is governed by others' bids and the predetermined minimum increment, to ensure you're the highest bidder until you win the bid or the bidding surpasses your maximum bid. In this way, you never pay more than the minimum needed to win the auction.

The bidding may never reach your maximum, in which case you have your bargain, since you're not required to pay your maximum bid. If the bidding surpasses your maximum bid, you can always place a higher bid, as long as the auction hasn't ended, or you can rest easy knowing you didn't overpay for the item.

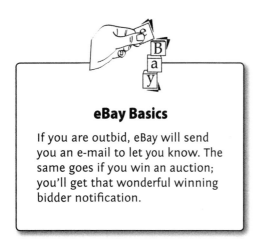

Many believe that proxy bidding is one of the most successful bidding strategies. It's simple, straightforward, and effective: you place your bid and you can walk away until the auction is over.

Bid Nibbling

Bid nibbling is a strategy that keeps you in control at all times—at least in as much you can be in control when dealing with computers and the Internet. Rather than placing your highest bid at the start and relying on the proxy system, you bid just enough to outbid the highest bidder. This entails diligence and a good bit of your time.

One side effect of bid nibbling that can give you a leg up is that if there are a few of you competing in this manner, the item's price increases early in the bidding process, and other potential bidders may be discouraged from joining the auction.

Sniping

Many eBayers agree that most of the auction action occurs within the last few minutes of the auction. They believe that a successful bidder needs to manipulate the last 10 seconds or so of the auction in order to win it. This is called sniping. The jury is still out on whether sniping is an ethical practice. But ethical or not, eBay allows it.

Sniping involves placing a bid as late as possible within the auction closing time, typically within the last few minutes or seconds of an auction. The underlying strategy is that your bid will go unnoticed, and competing bidders will not have a chance to reciprocate and bid higher since there isn't enough time left.

Helpful Tip

To increase your odds of being the highest bidder, look for auctions that end in the wee hours of the morning. Fewer people are awake and bidding during the nighttime hours, greatly increasing your chances of winning.

Sniping methods abound, but they fall under two categories:

> ➤ Manual: You sit at your computer during the last few seconds and input your bid by the conventional method.

> ➤ Automatic: You sign on with a web-based sniping service that will automatically place bids for you at specified times.

The downsides of manual sniping, even if you use a sniping software program, are enough to make you think twice about its efficacy:

> ➤ A slow or broken Internet connection can derail all your plans

> ➤ You're out of luck if your computer crashes.

> ➤ You're committed to sitting at your computer with your finger poised to hit that Place Bid button.

> ➤ Your hands are tied if you're interested in two auctions that are ending at the same time.

At first blush, automatic sniping seems to be the way to go. But it has some drawbacks as well:

> ➤ Most of the good websites are not free.

> ➤ You have to give your eBay ID information to these sites.

> ➤ The work is done by computers, which aren't flexible and can't strategize the way the human mind, flawed as it is, can.

No matter the method you use for sniping, your last-second bid could still be less than another bidder's highest bid. The take-home here is that neither sniping nor any other strategy will guarantee that you'll win an auction.

Research Your Competition

Although eBay keeps all identities private, it does provide ways to sleuth out a bidder's habits and trends. This can give you enough information to devise a strategy to squeeze out your competition.

On the listing page right above the Place Bid button is the number of bids the item has received. Click on that number and you'll see the bid history for that item. You can see how many bidders have been involved with this auction, the number of bids, the time left in the auction, and the duration of the auction.

Helpful Tip

Never try to bypass eBay and ask a seller to sell you an item on the sly. Besides losing the eBay Buyer Protection, your eBay account could be canceled. This is considered illegal in that you have violated your user agreement with eBay.

You'll notice that all the bidders have been given an anonymous name that is used throughout the auction to protect bidders' privacy. Next to this anonymous name in parentheses is the number of auctions the bidder has participated in and the appropriately colored star. Click on a bidder's anonymous name and you get the bid history for that individual.

Most illuminating is the 30-Day Summary and 30-Day Bid History. The 30-Day Summary includes:

➤ Total bids

➤ Items bid on

➤ Bid activity (%) with this seller

➤ Bid retractions in the 30-day period

➤ Bid retractions in the past six months

Here, you get a sketch of what type of bidder you're up against. The information gets more detailed in the 30-Day Bid History.

This information will clue you in on how experienced the bidder is, if he or she is an expert in the category or a collector (for instance, are all of his or her bids on antique furniture of a certain style, therefore the bidder is likely a serious eBayer and skilled at bidding), how often the bidder has participated in a seller's auction (again, sellers' identities are kept private and they are referred to as Seller 1, Seller 2, and so on), and the amount of time between the bidder's last bid on an item and the end of the listing (does this bidder snipe?). In this way you can get an idea of your rival's general bidding strategy and habits. Just remember all this information is available about you as well.

Implementing one strategy over another does not guarantee a win. Don't despair when you lose an auction. It doesn't happen often, but once in a while a winning bidder retracts his or her bid or the seller has duplicate items up for sale. In these situations, the seller can e-mail a Second Chance Offer to any of the other bidders who participated in that auction, offering to sell the item at a Buy It Now price equal to the bidder's most recent bid amount. You are not obligated to accept this offer, however.

CHAPTER 9

You Bid, You Won, You Conquered

In This Chapter

➤ What happens when you win an auction

➤ After the win

➤ The importance of feedback and communication

➤ What to do if you get the wrong item

In this chapter you'll learn about what happens after you've won an item. We'll take you through the steps necessary to pay for your item and get it shipped to you. You'll also learn what to do if you get the wrong item.

Winning Your Item

After surviving the bidding wars, you've finally procured your item. You were patient (hopefully) and you applied some bidding strategies and maybe even came up with some on your own. You stuck in there for the whole auction, keeping an eye on the prize without backing down. Maybe you even did a little sniping at the end. However you pulled it off, contractually you are the winner and upon payment the owner of the item in question.

So What Now?

After a seemingly long and grueling battle (or maybe you just chose Buy It Now), you were alerted via e-mail or text message that yours was the highest bid and you've won the item. If you were sniping, this won't be news to you, but if you placed a maximum bid and walked away, receiving this type of e-mail can be thrilling—especially if your winning bid was less than your maximum bid.

Both players in this transaction, buyer and seller, have responsibilities. As a buyer, there are motions you must go through before the entire transaction is complete, even some that are not a part of rules and regulations but are simply a matter of courtesy, netiquette if you will.

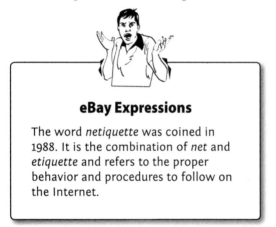

eBay Expressions

The word *netiquette* was coined in 1988. It is the combination of *net* and *etiquette* and refers to the proper behavior and procedures to follow on the Internet.

Imagine if it were as easy as paying for your item and going on your merry way. That's how it works at Walmart, but eBay is not exactly your local retail outlet. Once you understand the buying ins and outs on eBay, you'll get through this process in no time.

The first step many veteran eBayers take is to communicate with the seller and pay quickly for their item. This will reflect positively with the seller and make it more likely you will receive a positive feedback. So let us start with the communication.

Postgame

When you win an item, you are sent a congratulatory e-mail. Below the yellow banner exclaiming "Congratulations, the item is yours," is a note to you requesting payment and a Pay for It button. The e-mail continues with all the details pertinent to this transaction. Not that all the information on the page needs to be spelled out, because most of it is self-explanatory, here is some of the information you'll find on the page:

➤ The name of the item you bought

➤ The sale price

➤ Estimated delivery

➤ Shipping and handling

➤ Seller's user ID

➤ Seller's contact information

Now eBay steps aside and any further communications are between you and the seller.

Paying for Your Item

Once you've been notified that you have won the item you were bidding on, you need to pay the seller within three days using one of the electronic payment methods specified in the listing.

How quickly you pay greatly reflects on you as a buyer: the sooner you pay the seller, the more likely you'll receive positive feedback. PayPal, of course, is probably the easiest and quickest way to pay, and almost all sellers accept payment through PayPal.

Believe it or not, some people still do business using checks and money orders. These are still valid forms of payment, but delivery will be delayed since checks and money orders need to be mailed or shipped, and checks need to clear before the item is sent to you.

Helpful Tip

If you're going to pay with a credit card, don't do it via e-mail. Instead, give the seller all the pertinent information over the phone; it's a bit safer that way.

Paying by credit card, if accepted by the seller, is yet another way to go, but it's a bit riskier. Unfortunately giving out your credit card number leaves you open to identity theft. One way to minimize this risk is to do business only with top-rated sellers and PowerSellers.

Before pressing the Pay for It button, make sure you have the funds available to cover the payment. If you're paying with PayPal, be sure that there is more than enough money in your account or that you have a valid credit card or bank account registered with your PayPal account.

You don't want to finalize your payment without reviewing your order, double-checking that the item, price, any additional fees (shipping and handling, tax, insurance), and your shipping address are correct.

Now you're ready to pull the trigger, hit that check-out button, and be the proud new owner of an eBay purchase.

Helpful Tip

We live in a digital age, and although every digital document is a legal document, it is an important part of business to keep hard copies, paper records for tax purposes, for proof of purchase, and so on. Whenever you buy or sell an item, make a copy of the end-of-sale page, the e-mail, and any correspondences between you and the seller.

Leaving Feedback

The feedback process is essential to eBay's success. It consists of positive, negative, and neutral scores and allows for a brief comment.

The majority of transactions on eBay go well, and most feedback is good. But when a transaction doesn't go smoothly, you must be diplomatic about the feedback you leave for that seller.

At a restaurant, you tip according to the quality of service you get; in the same way, you give feedback on eBay according to the quality of service. However, unlike leaving a bad tip at a restaurant, giving a seller bad feedback can seriously damage his or her reputation. So use good judgment when leaving unfavorable feedback.

Let us go through the different feedback possibilities.

Positive Feedback

There are many factors to take into account when leaving good feedback. All sellers want good feedback, so they will make sure do whatever they can to ensure they get it. They will contact you quickly, pay for (buyer) or ship (seller) the item quickly, use the advertised shipping method (seller) they promised, provide delivery details (seller), ensure the item is exactly as described (seller), and bam—they've done everything they needed to do to get great feedback.

Then there are those who are well intentioned, but the transaction doesn't go exactly as planned. As a buyer, there are usually a few key points you need to keep in mind if you want good feedback:

➤ Pay quickly

➤ Communicate

➤ Take care how you leave feedback because it will dictate the type of feedback you'll get in return.

Before you leave feedback, take the following into consideration:

> ➤ Did this person contact you quickly following the end of the auction?

> ➤ Did the person ship your item quickly and provide you with a tracking number?

> ➤ Did the item get to you in the time it was promised? (If not, consider whether this is the seller's fault or the carrier's.)

> ➤ Did you get exactly what was advertised?

Keep these points in mind and leaving feedback will be a breeze.

eBay Basics

As of 2008, sellers cannot leave negative or neutral feedback about buyers. This decision was made so eBay transactions would be more akin to a traditional business relationship.

Negative Feedback

There are many reasons people leave feedback on eBay. Usually it's because we've had either a wonderful buying experience or a terrible one. Let's face it, each one of us likes things a certain way. What may be fantastic service to one person may be substandard to the next person. What one person considers in impeccable condition may be unacceptable to another because of the hairline scratch. You may even find people leave negative feedback for silly or vengeful reasons.

Once the auction has ended, the buyer and seller have three days to contact each other.

The questions asked in the previous section on positive feedback can be answered positively or negatively. If you are being honest and your answers to the questions above were negative, you are well within your rights to leave negative feedback. This is especially true, of course, if you did not receive the item that you won.

Neutral Feedback

Here is the infamous gray area. There are many things that can upset you about a seller's practices that may not necessarily be considered a violation. Perhaps the seller did not package the item securely, but the item was undamaged when you opened the package.

There are other slight deviations from a perfect A+++ seller that you may see. Someone may send you an item a day late. Another person may use a delivery service other than that which was guaranteed. If the overall outcome was relatively positive and deviated only slightly but to the point you feel the transaction doesn't warrant positive feedback, you can leave neutral feedback.

Helpful Tip

Many people hesitate to do business with sellers who have little or no feedback because they don't have a track record. Sticking with sellers who have a lot of positive feedback is one way to safeguard yourself against a transaction going wrong. But remember, these upstanding sellers started doing business without having any feedback, so not all newbies are bad.

Feedback Extortion

The feedback program has a great track record, but it has its ne'er=do-wells: people who use the fear of negative feedback as a manipulation tool. This is called feedback extortion.

Feedback extortion is essentially a threat to leave negative feedback if the seller does not acquiesce to an unreasonable demand or a demand that goes against eBay policy. Here is one scenario:

A person buys a video game. The game is shipped, received on time, and is exactly as described, but for whatever reason the buyer wants his or her money back. The buyer then tells the seller to release him or her from this obligation or else he or she will scar the seller's feedback score with negative feedback.

This is an extremely illegal practice by eBay's laws and eBay takes it quite seriously. So rather than caving in to feedback extortion, the seller can enlist eBay's help to mediate the dispute.

Detailed Seller Rating

As you read earlier, there is a Feedback Score you can click on that will take you to a seller's feedback profile. In this profile there is a neat little feature called the detailed seller rating. Here you are given four categories to rate on a scale of 1 (worst) to 5 (best) of a seller's eBay proficiency:

1. Accuracy of the item description: I find this a fairly silly category. As long as I have been buying eBay, I've pretty much received what was described in every listing. Some buyers are flexible and will allow for minor deviations, such as a slight scratch that the seller failed to mention but is hardly noticeable. Others would rate this seller negatively.

2. Satisfaction with the seller's communication: While many serious eBayers communicate immediately after a transaction, there is a grace period of three days. As long as communication occurs within those three days, the seller deserves a top score. Other points to keep in mind are the seller's professionalism and desire to make a happy customer out of the buyer.

3. The speed with which the seller shipped the item: This of course is a big deal. People want what they buy as soon as possible. Although it's wonderful when an item is received sooner than expected, a seller deserves a high score if he or she shipped the item during the allotted time stated in the listing. Things do come up, though, that is out of the seller's control. As long as the seller keeps the buyer informed and is doing everything possible to expedite the shipping, then the seller's score shouldn't suffer.

4. Reasonable shipping and handling charges: Sellers often charge for their time and packaging, and that's usually factored in the shipping fees. If a seller offers free shipping, the seller automatically gets a 5 star rating—you have no control over this. You also aren't allowed to rate this category if you picked up the item yourself.

Helpful Tip

Communication is paramount to the success of online auctions. The seller is responsible for detailing the item accurately, pointing out its defects and other detractions. However, the seller may not have mentioned one or two things that are important to you. Toward the bottom of the listing is a section where you can send questions to the seller. You can also see any other questions, and answers, that were asked by others.

Resolving Problems

Some people just don't play fair. Despite all the care you take to do business with the highest-rated, most upstanding sellers, you may end up dealing with one who's more interested in bucking the system and running with your money than with running a successful eBay business. You may find out the seller or the item doesn't exist, the seller sold the item to someone else, or the seller does not conduct him- or herself professionally.

Online Dispute Resolution

eBay provides access to SquareTrade, a dispute resolution provider. SquareTrade provides an online forum for individuals to resolve issues on their own. If that proves fruitless, SquareTrade provides a professional mediator, at a cost of $15, to see the process through.

Buyer Protection

Most items on eBay are covered by eBay's buyer protection, which covers the price of the item and shipping if the buyer doesn't receive the item or if it is not as advertised.

If the item hasn't been received and the seller hasn't been responsive to the buyer's e-mails, the buyer can open an eBay buyer protection case at http://resolutioncenter.ebay.com after the estimated delivery date or seven days after payment was made.

What to Do When You Get the Wrong Item

Mix-ups happen all the time. If instead of receiving your item you get something else, assume it was an innocent error and do what you can to find the source of the mix-up.

The first step you take is to contact the seller. In most cases the seller will do everything possible to correct the error whether, it is to refund your money or send you a replacement.

For those cases where the seller is unresponsive to your complaint, you can open an eBay buyer protection case.

Much of this seems like a lot of work compared to walking into a department store and purchasing an item. But problems are the exception on eBay, and you'll experience far more rewarding transactions than frustrating ones. eBay has protections and dispute resolutions in place to help make eBay a great place to do business.

CHAPTER 10

 **Selling**

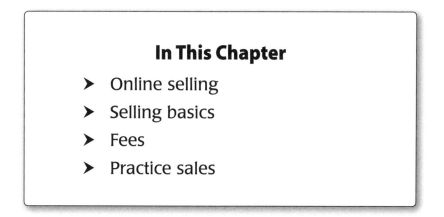

In This Chapter

➤ Online selling

➤ Selling basics

➤ Fees

➤ Practice sales

In this chapter you will be introduced to selling on eBay. You will learn about the various fees eBay charges for listings and how to get started by doing some practice sales. You learn about researching your item and getting to know your potential buyers and your competition.

Selling Online

As with any business, being successful at sales takes hard work and effort, creativity and ingenuity. Every seller has access to the same selling tools on eBay, but some are more successful at setting up a store and creating listings that sell. Some sellers work hard but make only enough profit to supplement their income, whereas others create a successful business and become millionaires.

So why isn't every seller a success? How is one person doing all the right things while others are doing all the right things even better? All the eBay selling tools are available to everyone; it's how you use and implement them that will greatly determine your success.

eBay vs Other Auction Sites

What's the big deal about eBay? Why would you choose to do your selling business on eBay as opposed to all the other similar sites on the Internet?

Other online auction sites just aren't as popular as eBay. These sites range from all-purpose auction sites like eBay to sites that auction specific items such as computer equipment. But eBay remains top dog, not just as an auction site, but as a site where you can create a viable and lucrative store.

eBay Basics

The eBay site offers eBay University and many individual tutorials to teach anyone who's interested every or just one or two aspects of doing business on eBay. Education specialists trained by eBay offer classes around the country as well. Go to eBay University in the Customer Support drop-down menu, click on Find a Class Now!, and follow the instructions to find an eBay class or instructor in your area. As with everything else eBay, check out the instructor's feedback rating.

Other online auction sites may have lower seller's fees or may specialize in the category of item that you sell, but none of them have the number of items and categories, specialty and regional sub-sites, membership, and exposure that eBay enjoys. A combination of custom selling options, management features, and buyer and seller protections make eBay the online auction of choice.

Now that I've tantalized your moneymaking palate, let's get down to the selling basics. Just how does selling on eBay work? Well, much like your first purchase, I am going to walk you through your first sale. But before we get ahead of ourselves we have to learn those basics. We don't want to dive in head first and find there is no water.

Selling: Getting Started

A surprisingly few supplies are needed to start selling on eBay. You probably already have most of the necessities:

> ➤ A computer: The more up to date the better

> ➤ An Internet connection: A high-speed connection (DSL or cable) is preferable

➤ A digital camera: A higher quality camera will take better pictures, of course

➤ Shipping supplies: Postal scale, boxes, labels, packing tape, packing material; have both generic (USPS) and UPS and FedEx shipping supplies on hand

To get started on the eBay website, you must be registered. If you've already been buying on eBay, you're already registered and don't need to reregister as a seller.

Once you're registered, you need to set up your seller account. Go into My eBay to confirm your personal information and set up an automatic payment method (usually through PayPal), which you'll need in order to pay seller fees and any reimbursements if claims are brought against you through the Buyer Protection Policy.

Although it's not much fun, becoming familiar with eBay's policies and procedures on selling is a good idea. Of course, you can't sell illegal items on eBay, but there are also some legal items you cannot sell on eBay and some that have certain restrictions. If you won't take the time to look at the whole policies and procedures section, then at least take a gander at what you can and cannot sell. You can find a complete list with explanations at http://pages.ebay.com/help/policies/items-ov.html.

Helpful Tip

I once knew a person who tried to sell Halloween contact lenses on eBay. There was nothing illegal about his lenses; they're sold at the corner boutique. But it turns out that eBay categorizes contact lenses under medical devices, which are prohibited. Make sure you know what is and is not allowed on eBay before you stock up on items to sell only to find out they're on eBay's prohibited list.

Nothing Is Free

eBay does a lot for us: it gives us a venue for buying and selling, it gives us protection, it acts as an intermediary for disputes. eBay is a business, and as such it charges for its services. Of course you don't get charged for window shopping or making a purchase on eBay, but you do pay a fee for using eBay as your vehicle for selling.

The four general categories of fees you may be charged for selling on eBay are:

➤ Insertion fee: A nonrefundable fee for listing an item; some listings do not require an insertion fee, and the seller doesn't pay for the listing unless the listing is sold

➤ Listing upgrade fee: Additional fees charged for adding upgraded features, such as Buy It Now and picture hosting, to the listing

➤ Final value fee: A fee based on a percentage of the total sales of the item, including shipping but not including sales tax if applied

➤ PayPal fee: Applies only if you do your financial transactions through PayPal

eBay Basics

The first fifty auction listings of the month are not charged insertion fees. Adding the Buy It Now feature to these fifty listings is free as well. The seller is charged a final value fee for each item, however, which is 9 percent of the total cost of the item not to exceed $250.

Within the general categories of fees are many types of specific fees that are charged for various other services and privileges. For a full account of seller fees, you can go to http://pages.ebay.com/help/sell/fees.html.

When you list an item, eBay tells you how much the insertion fee will be before you need to commit to the listing. But you are responsible for being aware of the other fees that you may be charged for.

eBay Expressions

The reserve price is a minimum price established by the seller but kept hidden from buyers. If the bidding doesn't reach or surpass the reserve price, the item doesn't sell.

Most fees are taken from the final price of the sale, and others are paid according to a specific billing cycle. Any unpaid fees can result in a hold on your entire eBay account. To find out what the final value and insertion fees are, go to http://pages.ebay.com/help/sell/fees.html#fvf_fixed.

Building Your Feedback Score

People are wary of any seller with little or no feedback. So it is a matter of great importance that you build up your feedback score. You'll find that a positive feedback score is one of your greatest assets when selling on eBay.

You can start building your feedback score as a buyer. If there isn't anything specific you want to buy, you can purchase a few low-priced items. Of course an astute buyer will notice your feedback score is based on buying, not selling, but at least this is a start. You will have to make a few sales for people to really start trusting you as a seller.

To get your toes wet and build your feedback score as a seller, practice by choosing a low-cost item to sell. Buyers are more likely to take a risk with a newbie seller when there is only $10 at stake. Establishing yourself prior to listing big-ticket items is the proper first step and will increase the chances of your success in the future.

Your Practice Sales

There is a sort of science to knowing what to sell, when to sell it, and how to sell it. Every eBay seller develops his or her own selling style. There is not one right or wrong way to sell on eBay.

Helpful Tip

There really is no set number of practice sales that you must make to be successful. The more you sell the more feedback you can accumulate. If you have the time and the merchandise, buy and sell low-cost items until you get a decent feedback score, one that is at least over 20.

While anything can be sold on eBay, there is no real demand for many items that are listed. But eBay takes to heart the saying, one man's (or woman's) junk is another's treasure. So if you have an empty bottle of 1921 Dom Perignon, and you're wondering who would want a champagne bottle with no champagne, think again. You can be sure someone wants it: perhaps a bottle collector or a wine collector who wants a bottle from the very first year Dom Perignon was bottled. Sometimes the more obscure items create furious bidding wars.

It's smart to start your selling adventure with something you own and no longer want. You may not have a one-of-a-kind collectible lying around the house or a diamond ring you no longer want, but your house is a treasure trove of items to sell.

Consider what people want and look around the house for items that may sell easily and quickly. It's best to choose a low-price item and one that won't be competing against thousands of other similar listings.

Here are some ideas:

> ➤ Kitchen: You probably don't see it right now, but the kitchen holds quite a few possible sellable items—that shiny four-slice chrome toaster, the seven-speed blender, the old percolator that used to belong to your grandmother. Even used items are worth something, sometimes more than you'd think. Remember, eBay started with the sale of a broken printer.

> ➤ Living Room: Televisions, stereos, DVD players, Blu-ray players, even wiring is worth something. You see those bookshelves in great condition in the corner? They can be broken down and sold. Furniture, area rugs, artwork, fireplace tools—all of these are potential sales items.

> ➤ Bedroom/Closet: Bedroom sets, vanities, picture frames, mirrors, and, of course, your closet: jackets, blouses, jeans, pants, shoes, baby clothes, the list is endless.

> ➤ Best Sellers: Electronic equipment like laptops, PCs, and monitors; CDs, DVD and Blu-ray movies, video games, and any collectibles you may want to part with such as signed baseballs or an impersonal autograph from an A-list celebrity. These are just some of the more desirable items you may have hanging around the house.

So I suggest when you are ready to embark on your first listing, open your eyes to what is around you. I guarantee you will start seeing sellable items in seconds. You can go to http://pages.ebay.com/sellerinformation/what-to-sell.html for more ideas.

Once you've chosen one or a few items you want to sell, you need to do your research. How many listings are on eBay for similar items? Will your item get lost in a crowd of similar listings? Is there something unique about your item that will make it stand out from the crowd?

Know Your Item

Just as buyers need to do their due diligence, so do sellers. You need to get a sense of the demand for your item, the prices similar items are selling for and have sold for on eBay, and typical shipping costs. How much is this item priced new and in pristine condition? What kind of discount is typically given for this item used and in the condition yours is in? Read the listings of similar items as though you were the buyer to get some insight into the buyer's perspective. What about the listing do you find compelling?

Checking completed listings, those that have ended in the last fifteen days, can give you a lot of information that will help you determine the demand for your item, choose the ideal price for your item, and create a winning listing. Completed listings include both those that have sold and those that haven't.

Search for your item by typing two or three keywords into the Search box found on most eBay pages and click Search. On the left of the screen where you can narrow your results, click on Completed Listings. Green represents those items that sold; red represents those that didn't.

Here are some details to look for and consider while you're doing your research:

> The category: Are there many categories in which the item can be classified? If so, did the item sell more successfully in one over the others?

> The title: Were there some titles that were more effective than others? Were certain key words used to help the item be more visible?

> The pictures: How many listings included a picture of the item; how many included many pictures? How effective were the pictures in helping the item sell?

> The description: Do some descriptions make a better sales pitch than others?

> The Format: Auction or fixed price; which format was more successful?

> The shipping method and cost: Is the item expensive to ship; do other sellers offer free shipping?

> The price: What were the opening prices? What price range did most of the items sell at?

Helpful Tip

The more you know about the item you're selling, the better and more compelling your item description will be. The year made, how the item was used (if it's an antique), famous people who owned a similar item—any tidbit simple or intriguing can set your listing above all the others.

Know Your Buyers

People from all walks of life are on eBay: some people sell items on eBay to help pay the bills or to supplement their income, some even making eBay their primary source of income reeling in thousands, even millions of dollars a year. People list cars, real estate, and other big-ticket items with a starting bid that is over $1,000,000. You will never find a more diverse demographic. The idea is to calculate the demographic for each and every item you sell, because no one item will draw the same bidders as the next.

Knowing who your buyers are will help you direct your sales pitch and determine the odds of an item selling at a given price. You can gear the way you present the item you're selling to the specific type of buyer or buyers who are likely to be interested.

Know Your Competition

Study your competitors. Every business, whether brick-and-mortar or online, keeps an eye on competitors, learning from their successes and their failures.

Study your competitors' listings. Is there a pattern to those who are successful and those who are not? Is there a standard that almost guarantees success? Check out the top-rated sellers and compare their styles to those of the sellers who get bad feedback. What are they doing right; what are they doing wrong?

Seller Protection

The Resolution Center exists equally for the protection of sellers as for buyers. Buyers can provide false contact information or claim they never received an item when they did. This could cost the seller relisting fees and other fees, as well as the forfeiture of the item if records weren't kept and the seller can't produce a tracking number to prove the item had been shipped. Vigilance and organization are prices both the buyer and the seller must pay to protect themselves against the unscrupulous. When that fails, there's eBay's Resolution Center.

CHAPTER 11

Listing Your First Item

In This Chapter

➤ Choose a listing form

➤ Create a simple listing

➤ Online auction or fixed price

➤ Payment and shipping

In this chapter you'll learn the ins and outs of creating a listing and begin developing your own listing style.

Creating a listing is considered an art to many eBayers. But an eye-catching, practically surefire listing is not easy to draft. It takes trial and error, research, observation, and much more. The time you take to perfect your listing technique will be time well spent and will pay off with high sales.

It may take a while for you to find your groove, but you'll have plenty of practice if you continue selling on eBay.

How to Begin

Many accomplished eBayers cannot remember their first listings, but it is probably the most important sale they ever made. A lot can be learned from your first selling experience by analyzing what it was you did that made the sale a success or a failure.

In Chapter 10, you selected an item or variety of items to launch your maiden selling adventure on eBay. You did some research on how similar items have sold on eBay and got to know your potential buyers and competitors. It's now time for you to create your first listing. Let's get started:

> ➤ Hover your mouse over Sell in the upper right of any eBay page to access the drop-down menu

> ➤ Click on Sell an Item. If you haven't already logged in, you'll be prompted to do so.

> ➤ On the Tell Us What You Sell page, fill in the box with the UPC, ISBN, or description of the item you want to sell

> ➤ Click on Browse Categories to choose the most appropriate category for your item. You can choose more than one category for a fee.

Helpful Tip

A good way to determine if your pricing is in line with that of other similar items, go to the Welcome Sellers page at http://cgi5.ebay.com/ws/eBayISAPI.dll?SellHub3&sellhub=&sellitem=&sellyouritemsignin=, write your item in the What's It Worth? box, click Look It Up, and you'll see the average price at which the item sold, the total sales in dollars, and the number of listings sold within the past seven days.

Selecting the category for your item is a very important part of your listing. A buyer who is browsing (as opposed to searching) has to choose a category to browse through. Most items can fit into a variety of categories; you want to choose the one that will raise the odds of your item being seen when a buyer is browsing.

Some more popular items such as cameras, CDs, and books are available in the eBay catalog and will appear as you type in your item description. In these cases, eBay automatically provides a barebones template that consists of a picture, a complete description and specs for the item, and the proper category.

You are required to list some items in the electronics category with the eBay catalog if your item exactly matches a product in the catalog. If you don't, your item won't get much exposure on the Search Results page and you may face other penalties such as your listing being removed.

Go to http://pages.ebay.com/sellerinformation/news/highlightingvalue.html to see a chart that gives you guidelines for listing with eBay's catalog.

Plenty of items are not listed in the eBay catalog. If this is the case with yours, you'll need to browse through the categories and choose the one that fits your item best. The research you did in Chapter 10 on completed listings would have given you some ideas on the more successful categories for your item.

You can list your item under more than one category, but it will cost you. To start, you may want to stick with one category. As you become a savvier, more experienced seller, you'll be able to determine on an item-by-item basis if the extra output of money is worth the extra exposure.

After you've selected a category, click Continue to be taken to the Create Your Listing page.

Create Your First Listing

eBay offers two formats for listing an item: the Keep It Simple form and the More Listing Choices form. For beginner sellers, the Keep It Simple form is the best option. This form allows you to create an auction-style listing and include up to four photos of the item. This option requires the following information:

➤ Title

➤ Photos

➤ Description

➤ Price and shipping costs

➤ Payment type

The More Listing Choices offers access to more selling formats and gives you other options. This form requests the same information required by the Keep It Simple form plus additional information, which includes:

➤ Subtitle

➤ Condition

➤ Brand (name of manufacturer)

➤ Listing designer

➤ Visitor counter

➤ Quantity of items

Of course, advantages and disadvantages of both forms abound and depend on each particular situation.

Helpful Tip

No matter which form you decide to use for your listing, the Keep It Simple or More Listing Choices form, you can change your mind partway through creating the listing by clicking on Switch To simple form or Switch to Form with More Choices, and the applicable data you've already entered will be transferred to the new form.

Continue creating your listing by completing the listing form. Options vary between the two forms, but in general the information required includes:

➤ Item title

➤ Description of the item

➤ Item specifics (depending on the category)

➤ Condition of the item

➤ Details of the item from the eBay catalog (if applicable)

➤ Item photos

➤ Selling format

➤ Starting price

➤ Listing duration

➤ Acceptable payment methods

➤ Shipping cost

➤ Return policy

eBay Basics

Don't forget to test any used item you're selling that has mechanical or electrical workings. If for some reason you're unable to test the item, you will need to sell it in as is condition, admit in the description that it hasn't been tested, or disclose that the item doesn't work if you have found that to be so.

Your Listing Title

The title, along with the photo of your item, is the most important part of a listing when it comes to attracting buyers. You want your listing title to be clear and descriptive, and because your title will be one among a sea of other similar titles, you want it to grab and hold the attention of buyers who are perusing their results pages.

Don't forget about the search engine, a behind-the-scenes worker churning away to bring up all listings that match keywords typed into the search box. When creating your title, keep keywords in mind.

eBay Expressions

Keywords are words a buyer is likely to use when searching for an item on eBay, or in any search engine for that matter. Keywords may include the manufacturer's name, important specs such as the number of storage terabytes in a computer, size, color—any word you think a buyer may use in a search for your item. You're allowed eighty characters in your listing title; make them count.

Dos and Don'ts of Writing a Listing Title

Before we get into some tips on how to write a great title, let's go over what not to do:

➤ Don't write your title in all capital letters. All caps are difficult to read and they make potential buyers feel as though you're shouting at them.

➤ Don't feel obligated to use all eighty characters that eBay allows for a listing title. If you're happy with your title and you haven't used all your allotted characters, don't "enhance" your title with meaningless words. No one includes the words *WOW* or *L@@K* in their search.

➤ Don't use punctuation or symbols such as an asterisk or a row of dollar signs or exclamation marks.

➤ Don't use keywords that do not relate to your item just to get buyers to your page.

➤ Don't create a title that is like all the other titles for similar listings. Find a relevant word or two that will attract buyers' attention.

Now here are some tips that will help you write a selling title:

➤ Do find a way to use the relevant keywords to make your title unique among other similar titles on the results page. A fun turn of phrase or play on words will draw buyers to your listing.

➤ Do look at titles of other similar listings for some ideas; you may even learn something about your competition in the process that may give you a leg up. By looking at completed auctions you can even glean which type of titles may have been most effective.

➤ Do know your item. Read the specs, manual, or any other information that you can find about the item. Incorporating specific details in your title will help you attract the buyers who are really interested in your item.

➤ Do check your spelling. If a keyword in your title is misspelled, your potential buyers may never find you.

eBay Expressions

eBay listing titles and descriptions are rife with acronyms, initialisms, and abbreviations. For a long list and definitions of eBay shorthand, go to http://reviews.ebay.com/Commonly-used-eBay-abbreviations-and-acronyms?ugid=10000000006694427.

Say Cheese

Your listing title paired with the photo of your item work hand in hand as a beacon to buyers. You've already crafted your informative, eye-catching title, now it's time to show your item in all its glory—from every angle.

Not just any old photo will do. Remember, you're advertising your item to get the highest price possible. For whatever reason, people are more interested in looking at a photo than they are in reading. No matter how good the listing title and description are, a horrible picture of a fantastic diamond may not sell as fast as a photographic masterpiece of a used car.

Digital cameras have made photography much easier and quicker than it was in days of yore when only film cameras were available. But showing your item in its best light still requires some planning and effort.

Taking Pictures

You're trying to make a sale, so you want to show off your item in its best light—figuratively and literally. Here are some tips for photographing your listing item:

eBay Expressions

The one free photo you can add to your listing is called a gallery picture and will be placed next to your title on the results page.

> ➤ Clean and shine your item to look its best.

> ➤ Make sure your photos are crisp and clear; your digital camera should be set at a high resolution.

> ➤ Make sure your photo is at least 1600 pixels on the long side.

> ➤ Take pictures of your item from many angles, especially if you're planning on adding multiple photos to your listing.

> ➤ Photographically note any spots that are damaged or flawed and highlight special features.

> ➤ Take advantage of natural light and make sure shadows aren't obscuring any part of the item.

> ➤ Place your item in front of a neutral backdrop that will help show it off.

Photo Editing

You don't have to edit your photo, but photo quality can make the difference between a buyer stopping to look at your listing or moving on.

First you need to upload your photos onto a computer. If you haven't done this before, refer to your camera's user manual for instructions. Once your photos are uploaded, save them with one of the following extensions:

> ➤ .jpeg

> ➤ .png

> ➤ .tiff

> ➤ .bmp

> ➤ .gif

Now you need photo editing software. You don't need to buy expensive software for editing your photos. Your computer may have come with a photo editing program such as Windows Live Photo Gallery or you can download free software from the Internet. The Standard

Uploader that eBay offers as a way to upload your photos to your listing also has editing options.

Here are some adjustments you may want to make to your photographs:

> ➤ Rotate the picture if necessary

> ➤ Crop out background "noise"

> ➤ Adjust color, contrast, and brightness

> ➤ Add your logo or member ID to a corner of your photo if your software has that function. This acts as a watermark and keeps other eBayers from using (stealing) your photo.

Adding a Photo to Your Listing

eBay allows you to add one photograph free of charge to each listing. You can add up to eleven more photos, but fees may apply.

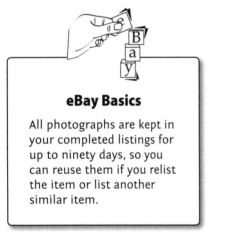

eBay Basics

All photographs are kept in your completed listings for up to ninety days, so you can reuse them if you relist the item or list another similar item.

Two types of photo uploaders are available to new eBay sellers:

1. Standard

2. Basic

The Standard Uploader is the default, but you need to have Adobe Flash Player 9 or above, or 10 and above if you want to use advanced features. If you don't have those programs on your computer and you don't want to add them, choose to upload your photos with the slower, less feature-rich Basic Uploader. You can go to http://pages. ebay.com/help/sell/pictures.html to see a chart of the different uploader options and what each has to offer.

Follow these steps to add photos to your listing:

1. In the listing form, go to the Bring Your Pictures to Life section and click Add Pictures. Here you'll be asked to install Flash Player if you don't already have it installed. You have the choice of clicking Basic to switch to the Basic Uploader, which doesn't require Flash Player.

2. Click Browse and open the folder on your computer where you saved your photos, select the photos you want to add to your listing, and click Open.

3. Click Upload. Your photos are saved in the Bring Your Item to Life with Pictures section.

The Sales Pitch

You've enticed buyers' interest with your listing title and photo—now it's time to clinch the sale with a sales pitch, otherwise known as the item description.

There is no right or wrong way to write an item description, but in most cases buyers will be looking for the following information:

> ➤ The brand, designer, manufacturer

> ➤ The model, serial number, style, vintage, edition

> ➤ Warranty and guarantee

> ➤ The item's condition—new, used, refurbished; works or doesn't work

> ➤ The size or dimensions

> ➤ The special features and flaws or defects

Many people feel that providing the buyer with detailed information is the best way to make a sale, but studies have shown that too much information on one webpage tends to lose the reader's attention. Your mission, then, is to master the art of saying a lot with a few words.

Some of the facts buyers want to know about an item don't have to be described in words because they're already obvious in the photos—the item's shape or color, for instance. If you photograph the item next to a well-known object like a coin or a ruler, you don't have to specify size or dimensions. And you don't have to discuss flaws if they're pointed out in the photos.

As you become more familiar and proficient with creating a listing, you'll want to try the more sophisticated options eBay has to offer with its More Listing Choices form to jazz up your description. You can also use eBay's Listing Designer (usually for a fee), templates, and HTML codes.

Helpful Tip

A helpful shortcut is to use the product details from the eBay catalog (if your item is in the catalog). And if you have any expertise relating to the item, include that in the description as well.

Selling Format

We're now at the point where you need to decide how you want to do business: what sort of selling format do you want to use in your auction. Refer to Chapter 10 for fees related to each format.

Auction-Style Listing

This is the eBay format we're all most familiar with: people bid for the item and the highest bidder wins. It can be the most exciting option if a bidding war heats up. You set the initial price, which shouldn't be less than the minimum you're willing to accept for the item. Use your previous research of demand for and typical price of similar items to help you choose a reasonable price for starting your auction.

You can add the Buy It Now option at a price that is 10 percent higher than the start price of the auction. This will likely attract more buyers to your listing.

You can choose how long an auction-style listing lasts:

➤ One day

➤ Three days

➤ Five days

➤ Seven days

➤ Ten days

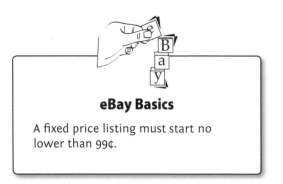

eBay Basics

A fixed price listing must start no lower than 99¢.

Fixed Price Listing

This selling format eliminates the auction. You set a fixed Buy It Now price and wait for someone who wants to by the item at the set price. At no additional cost, you can add the Best Offer option if you're willing to negotiate on the price. Multiple offers give you the opportunity to choose the buyer with the highest offer.

Just as with the auction-style listing, you get to choose among the following durations:

➤ Three days

➤ Five days

➤ Seven days

➤ Ten days

➤ Thirty days

➤ Good 'Til Cancelled

Payment and Shipping

As a seller, you can choose which payment methods you'll accept. Chances are you've already signed up with PayPal, but there are other avenues available to you:

➤ Bill Me Later (associated with PayPal)

➤ Credit and debit cards

➤ Paymate

➤ Payment upon pickup

➤ ProPay

➤ Skrill

For a breakdown of the pros and cons of each method, go to http://pages.ebay.com/help/pay/accepted-payment-methods.html.

The shipping costs and methods you choose are determined by what the research of your competitors turned up and the estimated costs of shipping.

If you haven't already, weigh and measure the dimensions of the ready-to-ship boxed item. Armed with this information, click on Research Rates to see what your shipping costs will be. Many sellers offer two shipping options: economical and expedited. Check the cost of each.

Don't seal the box until right before you actually ship. You'll want to include a packing slip and have access to the item if anything comes up, such as a question from the buyer.

You're almost done filling out your listing form. All you have left after calculating your shipping costs is to specify your return policy

Before you finalize your listing, read it through for thoroughness and accuracy, making any necessary changes, including correcting any misspellings you find.

Now you're ready to click List Your Item. You are now an official eBay seller!

CHAPTER 12

Sellers' Tools

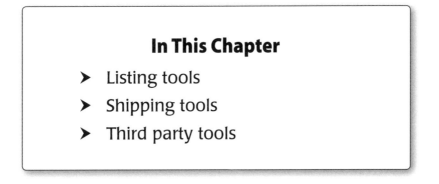

In This Chapter

➤ Listing tools

➤ Shipping tools

➤ Third party tools

You've listed your first item and have made your first sale—congratulations! You were successful using eBay's basic selling format. But you can do so much more with the additional selling tools that eBay brings to your computer. These additional tools can help you gain status as a PowerSeller or top-rated seller and can even grow your business so you can open your own eBay Store.

In this chapter you will cover some of the resources that are available to every eBay seller. eBay provides so many resources, which range from listing tools to buyer support, that we can't cover everything in detail here. You can go to http://pages.ebay.com/help/sell/advanced_selling_tools.html for more in-depth information.

Listing Tools

As you make more sales and become more comfortable with listing items with the basic form, you may want to graduate to the More Listing Choices form. This form allows you to customize your listing. You can choose colors, fonts, backgrounds, and so on. But if you really want to get serious, use eBay's Turbo Lister

Turbo Lister

Over the years, eBay has found better and more efficient ways to list items. One of the biggest and best creations has been a boon to everyone from people who list a single item to those who open eBay Stores. Turbo Lister is a free program that was created to facilitate listing and managing multiple items.

Turbo Lister is an offline program, which means that you can be on your laptop anywhere in the world and create listings for eBay without needing eBay or even an Internet connection. This allows you to create listings at your convenience and upload them when an Internet connection is accessible.

With Turbo Lister, you can do the following:

➤ Work with multiple listings, change formats or details, and use existing listings to create new listings

➤ Create and edit quickly using Design Editor

➤ Customize listings and control them using Listing Activity view

Of course as with any program, you need to be sure that your current computer meets at least the minimum system requirements for running the program. The requirements to install and run Turbo Lister are as follows:

➤ Microsoft Windows 2000, XP, Vista, 7

➤ Pentium II and above

➤ At least 250 MB free disk space, more than 500 MB recommended

➤ 128 MB RAM, more than 256 MB RAM recommended

➤ Internet Explorer v5.5 or later installed

eBay Basics

Unfortunately, Turbo Lister isn't available for Mac users at this time. For a fee, Mac users can consider third-party options such as www.garagesale.com or iSale at www.equinux.com/us/products/isale/index.html.

If your computer meets the minimum system requirements, you're ready to download and install Turbo Lister. Go to http://pages.ebay.com/turbo_lister/ and click Download Now. Follow the directions and soon you will have Turbo Lister installed on your PC to use anytime you want.

Follow these steps to set up Turbo Lister for the first time:

1. Open Turbo Lister.

2. Click on the Set Up a New Turbo Lister File option.

3. Enter your eBay ID and password.

4. Click on Synchronize to import your eBay listings if you have any; if not, click Create New Item (which is just like the Sell Your Item page).

To create a new listing, fill in the Create New Item form. This form guides you through the necessary steps for listing an item:

> ➤ Fill in the item title, subtitle, primary category, and secondary category

> ➤ Upload pictures

> ➤ Write a description or click Description Builder to help you format your description

> ➤ Use the optional Listing Designer, a pay-per-item option, to select fonts, colors, themes, borders, and to design the layout of your photos

> ➤ Select format (auction, fixed price, reserve, buy it now, quantity, and duration)

> ➤ Select listing upgrades if applicable

> ➤ Select shipping and payment options

> ➤ Preview the listing you've just created

> ➤ Save the item listing or save the listing as a template if you want it to be a master for additional listings

> ➤ Upload the listing to eBay

Helpful Tip

You can use eBay's Pre-Filled Item Information form to streamline your listing. Enter the UPC, ISBN, part number, or title, select the item that matches the one you're listing, and the form will generate a standard description you can use in your listing. This can be a great time-saver!

Turbo Lister offers an Inventory page that allows you to manage all the items you're selling on eBay. You can easily create new listings by duplicating similar listings or by using a saved template. You can edit a listing's details such as price or selling format, and you can even select multiple listings to change details on more than one listing.

You can upload your listings to eBay from the Inventory page by moving them to the Waiting to Upload area. This useful section allows you to do the following:

➤ Schedule the day and time for your listing to start

➤ Calculate listing fees

➤ Review listings

➤ Select one or many listings to upload

Once you've used Turbo Lister a few times, you will likely want to explore the additional features that it offers such as relisting unsold items and customizing.

Listing Management

eBay gives sellers many tools for managing their listings. Every seller should get to know these tools and take advantage of what they have to offer.

My eBay

You're already familiar with My eBay, but you probably haven't yet discovered what it can offer you as a seller. In My eBay, you can see and keep track of all your selling activity. You can customize My eBay, keep track of which items have been paid for and which have been shipped, and refer to your sales within the last sixty days. My eBay offers you many other seller tools as well. Just read on.

eBay Basics

Selling Manager supports all operating systems. You do need to have Microsoft Internet Explorer 6 or later, Mozilla Firefox 1.5 or later, or Apple Safari or later installed in your computer in order to use this this helpful tool.

Selling Manager and Selling Manager Pro

Selling Manager is part of My eBay and offers time-saving ways to do some of the administrative work in bulk. You can print labels and leave feedback in bulk. You can keep track of which of your listings require some action to be taken and automatically relist items.

Selling Manager Pro is a fee-based service used by many advanced sellers. It offers what Selling

Manager does plus more advanced business tools such as third-party-approved business apps. If you're a premium or anchor store subscriber, Selling Manager Pro is free.

Bulk Edit and Relist

This handy listing management tool in My eBay is a spreadsheet that helps you stay competitive by offering easy pricing adjustments, shipping services, and simultaneous revisions of listing fields for as many as five hundred live listings. As you build your inventory, Bulk Edit and Relist will be a very welcome tool.

Blackthorne Basic and Blackthorne Pro

Blackthorne Basic is a time-saving tool that helps you create professional-looking listings in bulk with help from its ready-made templates, track your listings, and manage your communication with buyers. Once you enter payment and shipping terms, for instance, it will automatically insert that information into multiple listings.

Blackthorne Pro is for high-volume sellers and offers the same tools that Blackthorne Basic offers, as well as the following:

➤ Inventory management

➤ Multiple user profiles

➤ Customized reporting

File Exchange

This is a free tool useful for high-volume sellers. A start-to-finish selling tool that, like Bulk Edit and Relist, allows a seller to list multiple items on eBay in a single file. It allows you to choose to list items using flat files from Microsoft's Excel, Access, or inventory software, and then transfer them to eBay.

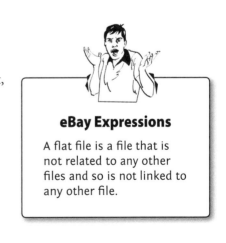

eBay Expressions

A flat file is a file that is not related to any other files and so is not linked to any other file.

To help you determine which tool will be more useful to you, go to the feature comparison table at http://pages.ebay.com/sellerinformation/sellingresources/featurecomparison.html.

Keep in mind that revising a listing may be somewhat restricted depending on a few factors such as the type of listing and the remaining duration of the listing. For more information about these restrictions, go to http://pages.ebay.com/help/sell/revising_restrictions.html.

Tracking Your Listings and Improving Your Sales

The best way to improve your sales performance is to track and analyze your listings. This would be nearly impossible to do without a handy program to synthesize thousands of morsels of information. eBay offers a few tools that do just that.

Listing Analytics

If you want to identify the listings that are your best and worst performers and the revisions that should be made to maximize your sales, eBay's free Listing Analytics app is the tool for you. You can even implement those revisions right from the app.

You can see how many people look at, click on, and purchase items that you've listed. You can even get tips on how to improve your listings and maximize your sales. In other words, the Listing Analytics app gathers and analyzes information from your listings, and then recommends steps you can take to optimize those listings. Very helpful!

Seller Dashboard

If you've received ten or more detailed seller ratings, you can take advantage of My eBay's Seller Dashboard. Here you can keep track of how you're doing as a seller, your status, ratings, and transactions from your very first sale to the present.

Sales Reports

This free tool helps you measure your sales performance against your sales goals. In doing so, it shows you what needs improving and what aspects of your listings are most successful. It ultimately helps you hone your sales strategy for best success.

Shipping Tools

Shipping is probably the part of the process that requires the most care since it involves the item leaving your possession. Packing and shipping can be time-consuming drudgery. But eBay offers a number of links to pages that will help speed the process:

➤ Links to pages where you can order shipping supplies

➤ A guide for choosing a shipping service

➤ My eBay offers discounted postage and label printing for USPS, as well as online payment

➤ A carrier and service options chart that can be found at http://pages.ebay.com/sellerinformation/shipping/chooseservice.html

> ➤ Automatic tracking information to both the seller and the buyer

> ➤ A comprehensive guide to ship[ping that can be found at
> http://pics.ebaystatic.com/aw/pics/pdf/eba219_shippingguide_final.pdf

eBay also provides many calculators to help you. Some of them are as follows:

> ➤ Shipping calculator to determine shipping rates

> ➤ Currency conversion calculator

> ➤ Combined shipping discount tool

Helpful Tip

Third-party shipping managers are plentiful; even the USPS has a tool on its site. Various tools can help you save up to 20 percent on shipping and cut as much as 50 percent from the total shipping time.

Buyer Support: Automated Answers

A seller's time could easily be monopolized by answering questions from buyers. And often the same few questions are asked over and over again, which is why eBay came up with Automated Answers and why every seller is opted in automatically. If you don't want to use the Automated Answers tool or otherwise want to make changes, you can manage your settings in My eBay.

eBay automatically generates questions and answers from the information you added to your listing, not including the information in the Sell Your Item form that's found under the Describe Your Item section. But if you have important information in that section, you can customize some auto questions and answers that you think may come up repeatedly.

One cool feature is that if you use eBay or PayPal shipping labels, Automated Answers supplies the tracking information.

You don't have to worry if a buyer has questions about eBay policy because eBay automatically provides answers to these questions.

Marketing and Merchandising: Stores

Once you've become proficient at selling on eBay and you've amassed a lot of listings, you may want to open an eBay Store. This tool helps you design, build, promote, manage, and track your online store and offers three levels of subscription to fit the needs of most types of business. You can read more about setting up and running an eBay Store in Chapter 14.

Third-Party Listing Tools

Sometimes eBay just can't offer everything everyone needs to be a successful seller. That's when third parties, businesses unrelated to eBay, step in with specialized tools to streamline tasks and add functionality to a listing.

To make sure these third parties are on the up and up, eBay has developed the Certified Provider Program as a way to qualify third-party developers and their tools. To compare providers you can go to http://pages.ebay.com/sellerinformation/sellingresources/listingsolutioncomparison.html to see eBay's comparison chart.

Auctiva

This is a very powerful listing tool. Boasting over 1,800 templates, this tool purports to rival Turbo Lister's features and power of listing management. Auctiva is quite proud of its easy-to-use one-page lister as well as a free cross-promotional scrolling gallery. Other Auctiva features include:

> ➤ Listing tools: free scheduling, auto re-list, and bulk live listing revisions tools
>
> ➤ Free marketing tools: Sellathon counter, auto-marketing e-mails, and auto-feedback tools

Helpful Tip

If you have some unusual selling method in mind, do some research—there may be a tool that does exactly what you want. For instance, there is a YouTube-based tool that helps you create a video to make your listing stand out from the rest.

Frooition

Specializing in providing website design services for eBay and other online channels, Frootion also provides software that helps you manage your eBay Stores, listings, and cross-promotions—all this without the need to have any understanding of HTML code.

Frootion boasts a proven track record of increasing eBay Store sales by as much as 30 percent with its custom eBay Store design and custom listing templates. With claims like that, I couldn't imagine not given this tool as shot, even if only for a short while.

Seller Sourcebook

This third-party tool is a tool that's easy to use for listing and image hosting. Sourcebook offers a flat-rate service to sellers that includes:

➤ Listings

➤ Coordination of listings

➤ Scheduling

➤ Cross promotions

➤ Large template gallery

With twenty-six tools to date, every eBay seller can find at least one that fits nearly any personality and selling style. Do yourself a favor and explore all the options.

Third-Party Selling Management Tools

Managing listings can be a full-time job. Don't wait until you have more listings than you can keep track of on your own. As you're building your business, look into the various third-party management tools that are at your disposal.

There are many tools to choose from, several of which have already been discussed because they act as both listing and management tools. Don't be surprised, then, if you find you already have listing management covered by having downloaded a listing tool. Turbo Lister, for example, is a fantastic listing and management tool.

Miscellaneous Tools

A tool exists for making nearly every aspect of selling on eBay easier and more efficient. The tools already mentioned are for the most important aspects. Below are tools that make certain steps in the selling process either less tedious, more effective, or both:

➤ Translation tool: Allows the listing to be translated into a different language; a great tool if you are going global

➤ Live chat tool: Allows bidders to chat with you live if they have questions about your item

➤ Photo tools: Various photo tools have different features depending on the developer, which may include custom-framing images in your gallery and using Flash.

➤ Feedback tools: These tools perform tasks such as sending automatic reminders to those who have yet to leave one, alerting you when feedback is left for you, as well as sending follow-up messages to feedback so buyers remember you and your courtesy

Check out these tools and others that are available, give them a try, and see which works best for you and your needs.

PART THREE

Advanced eBay

CHAPTER 13

 # Opening an eBay Store

In This Chapter

- ➤ How to treat your customers
- ➤ How to open and build your eBay Store
- ➤ How to manage your listings
- ➤ How to promote your store

In this chapter you will learn what it takes to become a PowerSeller and a top-rated seller, the importance of customer service, and you will create your very own eBay Store.

Customer Service

You may have the best products, with the most variety, or that are the hardest to find, but at the end of the day, you are simply a user ID on a screen. There are so many eBay sellers that it is nearly impossible to distinguish or remember one from another—unless you provide stellar customer service.

No seller is required to be a veritable cornucopia of hospitality, but even in the beginning stages of your building an eBay Store, providing good customer service will garner repeat business, more hits via referral from customers, and a respectable reputation. We have discussed the importance of feedback; the backbone of a positive, long feedback page is, indeed, customer service.

eBay Basics

It doesn't take a rocket scientist to know what it takes to provide good customer service: good communication. Don't leave your buyers in the lurch. Answer questions right away, send invoices and ship dates in a timely manner, and inform your buyers of any problems or delays.

Overall, customer service is a simple concept, but as an individual you can personalize the style of customer service you provide to reflect your business standards and ideals. If you pick out two eBay Stores right now and compare their feedback pages, you are likely find differences that point to each store's nuances. The owners of these stores worked hard to find their niche and are proud of what they have perfected.

PowerSellers and Top-Rated Sellers

A specific set of requirements needs to be achieved before being granted the status of PowerSeller or top-rated seller. Once achieved, the seller must maintain the requirements in order to keep the status. The status comes with benefits such as price breaks for listing and shipping fees, prominence in listings, and more.

eBay Expressions

A PowerSeller earns special benefits for reaching eBay sanctioned goals regarding account standing, volume of sales, positive customer feedback, and complying to policy.

A top-rated seller is a PowerSeller who receives even more benefits for accruing customer satisfaction ratings.

You can't grant yourself PowerSeller or top-rated seller status; you need to receive an invitation from eBay. And don't worry about membership fees—these programs are free.

Requirements

eBay recognizes sellers' achievements after evaluating multiple criteria every month to identify those who are eligible for the PowerSellers or top-rated sellers.

The PowerSeller program has tiers of membership, each with certain requirements that must be met and maintained. The basic requirements for all tiers are as follows:

> ➤ Have an eBay account for ninety days or more
>
> ➤ The account must be in good standing
>
> ➤ Feedback and detailed seller ratings (DSRs) requirements must be achieved and maintained
>
> ➤ The minimum volume of sales for the tier in question must be achieved and maintained
>
> ➤ Must be in compliance with eBay policy

From lowest to highest, these are the requirements you need to achieve in twelve months to become eligible for each tier of the PowerSeller program:

> ➤ Bronze: Must have taken in at least $3,000 in sales or completed 100 transactions with US buyers
>
> ➤ Silver: Must have earned at least $36,000 in sales or completed 3,600 transactions with US buyers; must offer twenty-four-hour e-mail and phone support from 6 am to 10 pm
>
> ➤ Gold: Must have taken in at least $120,000 in sales or completed 12,000 transactions with US buyers; must offer twenty-four-hour e-mail and phone support from 6 am to 10 pm; must offer some level of specialized account servicing
>
> ➤ Platinum: Must have taken in at least $300,000 in sales or completed 30,000 transactions with US buyers; must offer twenty-four-hour e-mail and phone support from 6 am to 10 pm; must offer some level of specialized account servicing
>
> ➤ Titanium: Must have taken in at least $1,800,000 in sales or completed 180,000 transactions with US buyers; must offer twenty-four-hour e-mail and phone support from 6 am to 10 pm; must offer some level of specialized account servicing

These are the basics. You can get more detailed information by going to http://pages.ebay.com/sellerinformation/sellingresources/powerseller_requirements.html.

Helpful Tip

Even if you already have high-volume sales, you may want to start with the Basic Store subscription so you can experience trial and error in a more stripped-down format.

Opening an eBay Store

Opening an eBay Store is no small challenge. Thankfully, eBay has a tool that can help you create your store. This invaluable tool walks you through the steps of building your store, managing your listings, and promoting your store.

You have a choice of three types of store to subscribe to:

1. Basic Store

2. Premium Store

3. Anchor Store

To help you choose which type of store would be best for you, eBay has put together what it calls the Fee Illustrator. Go to http://pages.ebay.com/sellerinformation/news/FeeIllustrator. html, fill out the form, and click Calculate.

Once you have eBay's idea of your perfect store subscription based on your selling activity, go to http://pages.ebay.com/storefronts/subscriptions.html to see what the fees are for each type of store.

In general, eBay recommends the following:

➤ Basic store: List more than 50 items a month or have a high volume of auction-style listings; have a PayPal account and are PayPal Verified

➤ Premium store: List more than 250 items a month in fixed price listings; list in both fixed price and auction-style listings; have a PayPal account and are PayPal Verified; have a standard or above standard performance rating (go to http://pages.ebay.com/help/policies/seller-non-performance.html to read about the performance standards)

➤ Anchor store: List a high volume of fixed price listings each month; have a PayPal account and are PayPal Verified; have a standard or above standard performance rating

When opening a small business, there are many questions that come to mind, such as what the name of your business will be or what color you will paint the walls. Although an eBay Store is a business in cyberspace, most of the questions will still apply in one form or another. For instance, you have no walls to paint, but you need a color scheme for your online storefront.

Choose Your Subscription

With everything decided, go to the Build Your Store page at http://pages.ebay.com/storefronts/building.html. This page shows you the basic and advanced layouts. It also gives you some design examples of a few successful eBay Stores.

After you've browsed the layouts and the example success stories, click Manage My Store in the upper left of the page. This takes you to a page where you can choose your subscription level. Basic caters to all beginners and is a good place to start, even if you do sell at high volume. Continue by following the instructions. Once you hit Submit, an email confirmation will be sent to you with confirmation and the URL of your eBay Store.

Building Your eBay Store

Before you begin building your eBay Store, think about what you will primarily sell, and what type of "personality" (lighthearted and funny, serious, personable, straightforward) you want to give it. Think about designing a logo and theme to match your store's ambiance.

Helpful Tip

When choosing your store's color theme, keep in mind that different colors can evoke different moods. For instance, blue evokes tranquility, yellow evokes happiness, and gray evokes wisdom. Choose colors that best represent the feeling you want buyers to get when they visit your store.

You can design and customize your store fairly quickly using a tool called Quick Store Tuneup. You can get to the Tuneup page from either the eBay Stores Overview page or from the Congratulations page you are taken to after creating your store. Once you are there, you are given the opportunity to edit the following:

➤ Store color and theme: Choose the color of your store pages and choose from several pre-created themes.

➤ Store description: Use keywords to accurately convey what you sell. Wow your potential customers and summarize your store in a neat little paragraph.

➤ Item display: Choose the layout and sort order of the items that will be listed.

➤ Promotional boxes: Choose whether or not you want these neat little boxes that help buyers find items and information to your store.

➤ Store Marketing: Opt in for e-mails to be automatically sent to new subscribers and for marketing e-mails about your newsletter.

Personalizing Your Store

Although the Quick Store Tuneup is a handy tool for getting you started with your eBay store right away, you can make so many more changes to your store than it allows.

Go to Manage My Store. You can get there from My eBay now that you have a store. In Manage My Store you have the ability to customize your store any way you choose.

On a panel on the left of the Manage My Store page you will find every link you need to create a store that is unique and yours. From the Store Design panel you have the following links:

➤ Display settings: Your eBay Store can have any look to it you'd like, and this is where you begin. The color, theme, overall feel of your store can all be created and edited from here.

➤ Store categories: You can have up to three hundred categories and subcategories. While most people choose to have a general theme and stick to a certain inventory, you could potentially have a selection of hundreds of different types of merchandise.

➤ Custom pages: Here you can create, edit, or delete pages, or you can change the order of page links in the Navigational Bar. Your pages will adhere to the layout of the custom page you create.

➤ Promotion boxes: You can create boxes inside your pages that you can use to highlight featured items, announce specials, or provide alternative ways for buyers to browse in your store.

➤ Search engine keywords: Keywords that best describe your store and are most likely to be used in a buyer's search.

➤ HTML builder: You do not necessarily need to use this but for those who want to separate themselves from the other stores and certainly from non-store owners, HTML is the way to do it.

To create a store that suits you and attracts business take the following into consideration:

➤ Decide on a color scheme

➤ Create a logo for your store

➤ Create categories for the various items you'll be selling

➤ Create a store description that will entice would-be shoppers

➤ Decide how you will use the promotional boxes

HTML

HTML is far from being new. It is a markup language that is the foundation of web pages all across the Internet. It's straightforward enough to learn on one's own, but it is also taught in schools throughout the United States and abroad.

You may have heard HTML at one time or another described as a programming language. By definition, a programming language is a series of commands that governs what a machine or program will ultimately do. HTML does not fit that category. HTML is a markup language, a translator, if you will. It is simply a way to tell a browser to convert, or translate, a series of tags (codes) into the brilliant websites you see everywhere on the Internet.

The tags are made up of commands surrounded by angle brackets (<>), which determine the appearance of the web page, including the font, color, headings, and references to other web pages. These codes are interpreted by Internet browsers, which create the design of the page we see on our computer screens. If you were to look at the HTML form of any website, odds are it would like gibberish to you. But when you allow an HTML generator to do its "magic," you have the website you recognize.

Keep in mind that you cannot use HTML in just any place you type. You must specifically be typing in an HTML editor, which will translate the tags. Luckily, eBay provides an HTML editor where you create your listing.

Let's take a look at HTML tags for fonts:

➤ <FONT size=4>: This is a tag that indicates the size of the font you would like to use. Keep in mind that the HTML size of font does not correspond with font sizes in a word processor.

➤ <FONT size=4 face=Arial>: This tag indicates not only the size of the font, but the font type as well.

➤ <FONT color=ff0000>: As you can imagine, this tag indicates color. I used the first color code that came to mind.

> ➤ <p>: This indicates the beginning of a paragraph

> ➤ </p>: This indicates the end of a paragraph

Other such HTML elements and tags include:

> ➤ <tr>: This tag defines a row in an HTML table.

> ➤ <td>: This tag defines a standard cell in an HTML table.

> ➤ <th>: This tag defines a header cell in an HTML table.

Helpful Tip

You can get a chart of HTML codes that are frequently used on eBay by going to http://pages.ebay.com/help/sell/html_tips.html.

Much like anything else in business, you will need to play around with HTML to perfect and develop your style.

Here are a few tags to give you an idea of what HTML looks like:

> ➤ <h1>This is a heading for this chapter</h1>: This is how you would write your heading.

> ➤ <p>This is a paragraph for this chapter</p>: This is how you would write a paragraph.

Here is how you write a link in HTML:

<a href="http://www.ebay.com">eBay World's Largest Auction Website</a>

The words "eBay World's Largest Auction Website" is the hyperlink you will see on your webpage. But it will take you nowhere without "<a href="http://www.ebay.com">," which is what tells the editor that the link must go to that URL.

Overall, HTML is incredibly easy to pick up. Unlike a computer programming language, it requires no knowledge of computers, programming, math, algorithms, or anything else at an advanced level. All that is required is tenacity, the desire to perfect your own style with the tools that are so readily available.

Helpful Tip

Websites that teach HTML abound. I refer people to www.w3schools.com because it not only shows every possible HTML tag, but it also gives a brief explanation of each one. Then it provides an HTML editor for you to use to practice everything you learn.

Now you're all set up and ready to start business. Running an eBay Store, as with any other business, requires hard work and ingenuity. You have opened a business and should take advantage of registering your store as a business on eBay. Go to the Registration page and click Want to Open an Account for Your Company.

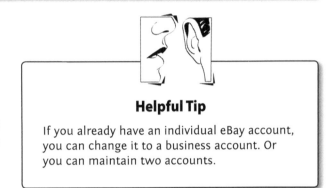

Helpful Tip

If you already have an individual eBay account, you can change it to a business account. Or you can maintain two accounts.

Manage Your Listings

Now that you have an eBay Store, you must manage your listings more efficiently. You should be constantly aware of what's going on with every one of your listings. The various listing tools offered by eBay are discussed in Chapter 12.

One of the Selling Manager views keeps track of your listing activity, such as scheduled listings, active listings, and listings that have ended. The Activity Log gives you a comprehensive overview of all activity going on in your eBay store.

It may seem a little daunting at first, but once you get the swing of it, managing your listings in your eBay Store will become easier, and you will be tracking your listings in every stage of the auction process with relative ease.

Promote Your Store

You've put all that hard work into planning and building your store. You're open for business and it's time to get the word out. To grow as a business, you need to promote your eBay Store.

There are two venues where you can promote your store: on eBay and off eBay. Let's start with promoting your store on eBay.

Promoting on eBay can be done in a number of ways.

Cross-Promotion

This is a powerful and useful tool that allows you to advertise items you currently have listed on other listings. Buyers see up to twelve of your listed items when they bid on one of your auctions or click on Buy It Now.

eBay Basics

You can change settings so you can cross-promote your items in more areas. Just go to My eBay and click Marketing Tools. On the left of the page, click Settings.

Cross-promoting is set as the default, but you can change the criteria for which items are used for cross-promoting. This is a powerful tool and using it could send your sales soaring.

Promotion Boxes

Promotion boxes can be used to highlight items, advertise special offers, and more. You can showcase various items on any page, advertise upcoming store events, newsletters, pretty much anything you would like to promote. You can customize the box to your liking and edit it in the best way you feel will get your promotion noticed.

Go to My eBay, click on Manage My Store, then click on Promotion Boxes on the left side of the page. Don't overlook the wide range of settings this tool has to offer.

Custom Store Header

Use this simple tool to create a custom header for your eBay Store. You can select from four different templates to promote your featured items and highlight one or more sub-featured items in one of four ways. Choose the layout that you feel looks best. You can also change the colors of the header as you see fit.

Customize Checkout and Payment Information

This is the last stop for buyers, which also makes it your last opportunity to promote one or more items and your store. The Checkout page shows your store logo, a custom message from you, and one or more items. This same information will also be sent in the form of an e-mail. Make sure to create a message that not only thanks buyers for their business, but also attempts to pique their interest in other items you have listed.

Markdown Manager

There's nothing like a good sale to create excitement around a store. The Markdown Manager tool promotes special savings in your store and in your fixed price listings. You can access it under Marketing Tools.

There are many ways to promote your eBay Store outside of eBay. Here are some that eBay recommends.

Helpful Tip

If you send out newsletters, promote your sales by sending e-mails to your newsletter subscribers.

E-mail Marketing

Trigger repeat sales by sending newsletters and sale notices to people who have made purchases at your store using E-mail Marketing. You can send up to 10,000 free promotional e-mails each month, depending on your eBay Store's subscription level. Additional e-mails are just 1¢ each.

Stores to Go

You can advertise your store and your store's listings outside of eBay by adding the Stores to Go widget to your blog, website, and social networking site. This widget displays your store, some listings, and a convenient little search engine to look for specific items the store may have. It is a handy tool and can certainly increase your sales.

You can find creative ways to use this tool. For example, you can add it to your social networking pages, but why not create another page under your store's name for the sole purpose of promoting your store and attracting complete strangers. You host discussions concerning your items and sales. That is simply one way to get creative with a tool eBay offers.

Search Engine Optimization

Search Engine Optimization (SEO) is an incredibly important and low-cost method of drawing buyers to your eBay Store. By employing certain SEO methods, you will get the most hits out of search engines as you possibly can. Here are just a few most-used SEO methods:

➤ Store name: Your store's name determines its URL. Choosing a store name that describes what you sell will make you more visible in searches.

➤ Store description: Keep in mind that the more specific your store description, the more keywords you use, the better the chances are that your store will show up in searches. Make sure your description accurately conveys your inventory.

➤ Custom categories: If you have custom categories, make it much easier for people to find your store using a search engine by ensuring you do not choose vague names for the categories.

➤ Unique identifiers: A surefire way to increase your store's visibility on a search is to use unique product identifiers when applicable. These include UPCs, ISBNs, and Manufacturer's Part Number (MPN).

➤ Character usage: Take care to use the character allotment wisely. Do not use empty words like *wow* or *look*; people don't search for words like that. Make sure your store name and description steer clear of words like these.

➤ Keyword management: You can and should customize your keywords in Manage My Store to improve your store's rankings in search engines using the same principles from SEO. Primary keywords should be the best keyword you can think of for a specific page and secondary keywords should act as very good runner-ups to the primary keyword.

➤ RSS feeds: An RSS feed sends out regularly updated summaries of the most recently listed items to subscribers of your store.

Other promotional methods include those used away from the computer. You can create some promotional flyers and pack them in your shipments. The flyer should include your logo, store name, and contact information.

Customized stationery is a great way to promote your store. Business cards, letterheads, envelopes and other traditional business stationary are all useful promotion tools.

So you now have an eBay Store to call your own. This is just the beginning of what will hopefully be a long and fruitful endeavor.

CHAPTER 14

 # Inventory, Budgeting, and Marketing

In This Chapter

➤ Building inventory

➤ Creating a budget

➤ Determining your expenses

➤ Getting the word out through marketing

In this chapter we will be discussing the basic business strategies, such as budgeting, keeping inventory, and marketing, that one would need to run an eBay Store.

Inventory

It was enough to buy inventory as needed when you were doing a low-volume business, but now that you have an eBay Store, you need to have enough inventory on hand to match the volume you expect to move. To manage your store, you will need a system to keep track of your inventory.

Keeping Track of Inventory

Tracking inventory is an essential part of every business that sells merchandise of any kind. Owning (whether by buying or by downloading freeware) an inventory tracking program is crucial. There are so many out there and while there are programs that are highly rated, they are also very expensive and may be more than you actually need. Since you're just starting out, freeware will do nicely.

One of the first steps once you get the software is to enter each and every item into your software program. If you have multiples of an item, list each one separately. Give each item a unique identifier. This is important for search engine optimization and optimum exposure. Each item listed should have the ideal price and a description (specs, condition of item, etc.).

Whenever an item sells, update the program to reflect that the item is no longer in inventory, place the item info in the restock part of the program, input the final sale price, and move on to the shipping part of the selling process.

Stocking and Restocking Inventory

There are several ways to stock inventory. After you have some experience under your belt, you will perfect your own methods based on your store and your merchandise.

One way to accrue and stock inventory is to look for great deals on eBay. Another method is to buy from a wholesaler either online or in-store.

Helpful Tip

It is a good idea to purchase inventory, point-of-sale, or accounting software. While eBay provides tools, such as the features in Turbo Lister, streamlining your business with a third-party program dedicated to inventory control will not only keep your business in order, but it is also a step toward becoming a true entrepreneur.

Initially it may take a few weeks to completely stock your shelves. After that, a good restocking schedule will consistently keep you on track.

Remember that to get to PowerSeller level, you need to reach a certain volume of sales. Not every item will sell, so your goal should be to have more inventory than you need to reach that PowerSeller quota. The sooner you get to the first PowerSeller tier, the sooner you can restock and make it to the next tier, and the sooner you can reach top-rated seller status.

Schedule time to go over inventory, create deadlines, and set goals. Review the previous day's, week's, or month's sales reports; create listings for new items; and set aside time each day or week to shop for new inventory. Setting aside time each day to focus on your eBay Store ensures tasks get completed and goals are reached.

Helpful Tip

Never begin creating a listing for an item before you have it in hand. Even if you have already purchased the item, don't list it until it is in your hands. Too many things can go wrong. You could receive the wrong item, the item might not be exactly as described, it could get lost in transit or simply be detained due to a hitch in transit. Any one of these scenarios could derail a listing, causing a domino effect that leads to unhappy customers and negative feedback.

As each item sells, update your inventory records and determine if the item is hot enough to add to your restock list. It's a good practice to check your restock list every morning and begin shopping for whichever items are on the list. If possible, buy your items in bulk to save money on per unit costs and shipping, and to take advantage of any bulk rate discounts that may be offered.

eBay Basics

When moving small volume, high profit is ideal; when moving large volume, any profit is good. It simply becomes a matter of moving merchandise. Moving merchandise at a high buy-sell margin becomes the best way to generate higher revenue.

Inventory Storage

Every retail business has to decide how and where it stores its merchandise. Department stores usually have a stock room; other businesses may rent out warehouses to store their inventory. Neither of these options is likely right for you.

In the beginning, you'll probably store your inventory in a spare room, basement, or garage. However, at some point you may be moving such a volume of merchandise that you may not have the room in your home to store it all. Then renting a storage unit or office space becomes a very possible solution.

Your store may grow from an easily run home-based business to a complex store selling hundreds of items in a multitude of categories. You will then join the legions of eBay sellers who rent office space, storage space, and shipping space. You actually may even end up running an adjunct brick-and-mortar store, as well as your online eBay Store, to manage and sell through all your inventory.

eBay Basics

Most PowerSellers who have reached platinum level rent warehouses where they store their inventory of hundreds (if not thousands) of items, because when you are making thousands of transactions a month, your little garage is not going to cut it.

Budgeting

Many business fail because of bad accounting. The best way to avoid this disappointment is to create and adhere to a budget. If you feel this part of running a business is a bit over your head, hire an hour or two of an accountant's time to set you off on the right track.

Set aside a percentage of your budget for your recurring expenses such as the following:

➤ Overhead

➤ Insertion fees

➤ Final value fees

➤ Inventory

➤ Marketing

How you set up your budget should be based on your experience, your sales volume, and typically by your own trial and error. It is best to begin slowly and err on the side of caution.

Budgeting for Overhead

Your overhead is the cost of everything needed to run a business, recurring operating costs that the business cannot do without.

The overhead of an online store includes expenses such as the following:

➤ Selling costs

➤ Monthly store dues

➤ Inventory

➤ Shipping materials

➤ Postage

Your expenses as an online business owner are certainly less than those of a department store. Even so, your overhead costs will certainly take a bite out of your wallet.

eBay Expressions

Overhead is the amount you spend on the expenses needed to run a business. For brick-and-mortar stores, overhead includes rent, utilities, and salaries.

When your business has grown to the point that you need to rent office and/or warehouse space, make sure it is efficiently run and match your volume in terms of rent.

Budgeting for Marketing

What good is a store if no one has heard of it? A decent budget should be allocated to getting the word out about your store. At first you may want to go with low-cost marketing such as e-mail lists and electronic newsletters. And don't forget the free marketing tools eBay has to offer.

Budgeting for Shipping Materials

You want to be sure you're well stocked with shipping materials. Once that sale is made, you want to get the item to the buyer as quickly as possible. Frequently positive feedback depends on the speed by which buyers receive their eagerly awaited purchase.

Helpful Tip

You can print shipping labels through My eBay. When you use this service, an e-mail stating that the item has shipped is sent to the buyer, and tracking information is automatically updated in My eBay. Good customer service can make or break a feedback score. Go to ebay.com/shipping for a full account of the ins and outs of its shipping services.

Some shipping services offer free materials; others charge a minimal fee. And don't forget about the shipping services eBay offers.

Shipping materials include the following:

➤ Boxes

➤ Packing tape

➤ Styrofoam popcorn

➤ Bubble wrap

➤ Envelopes of various sizes and padding

Expenses

Most of your expenses will be associated with your overhead. As time goes by, you will find ways to cut your overhead budget without compromising your business. Among the overhead expenses are:

➤ Keeping your eBay account up to date and paid for

➤ Applicable final value and insertion fees, etc.

➤ Keeping your inventory stocked (this makes up a good chunk of the expenses)

➤ Marketing

Many more expenses can accrue. You, as a businessperson, will have to adequately allocate monies to different expenses while keeping an eye on your budget and profits.

Running an online eBay Store makes for low overhead and high profits at first. But your business acumen is tested when you begin moving heavy volume and find yourself needing to rent a store or warehouse. You may find yourself expanding your inventory immensely.

Helpful Tip

It is a good idea to take a portion of your profits and reinvest it in your business. You may be able to increase your efficiency (thereby your profits) by investing in your own postage scale, for instance. Reinvesting in your business will help it grow.

Your expenses will go through the roof, but if you manage your store efficiently, you can do all this and successfully turn a profit.

Marketing

No company can thrive without getting their name out there. The super mega-mart can afford circulars, mailers, commercials, radio ads; in short, it can spend millions of dollars in advertising. It even has an advertising firm specifically hired to do the marketing for it.

Now here we are, a small up-and-coming eBay Store. Online stores use different advertising techniques than brick-and-mortar stores use. As mentioned earlier, eBay offers marketing tools, which relate to the needs of the online store.

How you market strongly depends on what your revenue stream is. If you are selling ten items a week, setting aside a marketing budget is not feasible. But those who own an eBay Store or are PowerSellers or top-rated sellers should absolutely spend some time, energy, and money on marketing.

Marketing methods can be altered depending on how much you allocate toward your marketing budget. This is where your business acumen comes into play. You look at your volume, decide how much you should spend on marketing based on that volume, and take it from there.

You can also market your item in quieter ways. For example, eBay's Gallery Plus, in which you can hover your mouse above a listing photo and it becomes enlarged, as well as many other marketing tools give your item a better chance of selling. It is also something you must factor in when considering your budget. All in all, marketing is a large portion of a business's budget and monies need to be allocated for it monthly.

It will become evident either through your own process or by research that different businesspeople conduct themselves differently but the major points of businesses are never veered from. If you are going to be a successful businessperson, you must find your financial balance, and only then will you find success.

CHAPTER 15

Trading Assistant

In This Chapter

➤ The Trading Assistant Program

➤ Becoming a Trading Assistant

➤ Registered eBay Drop-Off Location

In this chapter you will learn about an alternative to selling items on your own or through building an eBay Store. You will learn about the Trading Assistant Program and all that it involves. Whether you want to be a Trading Assistant or want to use a Trading Assistant, you'll want to read on.

What is the Trading Assistant Program?

As you know, eBay is an online auction site dedicated to bringing buyers and sellers from all over the world together. It acts as a proxy, an intermediary, a broker, to those who want to buy or sell. It is a place to make money.

eBay Expressions

A Trading Assistant is an independent businessperson who must be a US citizen, abide by all of eBay Trading Assistant rules, sell ten items or more every three months, and have a feedback score that never drops below 98 percent positive.

Some people would love to get involved in selling on eBay and making a little extra money, but either they don't have the time, don't care to learn how to become an eBay seller, or don't want to deal with buyers and the hassle of shipping. So eBay came up with the Trading Assistant Program.

Helpful Tip

You can supplement your income simply by hiring a Trading Assistant to sell your unwanted or outgrown household items, and then do nothing but sit back and collect your share of the profits.

The Trading Assistant Program takes those who have items to sell but do not have the time or knowhow to sell them, and pairs them with experienced eBay sellers who are more than willing to help them list and sell their items.

What Exactly Is a Trading Assistant?

A Trading Assistant acts somewhat like a consignment store. The Assistant takes your items to sell at an agreed-upon price for an agreed-upon percentage of what the items sell for. The main benefit of using a Trading Assistant is that you get an experienced eBay seller to do all the work of listing and selling your item, and you still make a bit of extra money without sacrificing a lot of time and effort.

There are two types of Trading Assistants:

➤ Registered eBay Drop-Off Location: These Trading Assistants provide a drop-off location that is staffed and has its business hours posted. You take your goods to the drop-off location, or some Trading Assistants offer pickup services.

➤ Trading Assistant on eBay: Most of these Trading Assistants come to you to assess and pick up your goods, and some also provide drop-off locations.

How It Works

If you are a seller looking for a Trading Assistant, follow these steps:

1. Go to the Trading Assistant Program home page at http://pages.ebay.com/tahub/index.html

2. Search for a Trading Assistant in your area by clicking Find a Local Trading Assistant to Sell for You

3. Click on Find a Local Trading Assistant Near You.

4. Fill in the boxes with your location and follow the directions for any of the options offered.

5. Click Search and get your list of Trading Assistants in your area.

From the list of Trading Assistants in your area, you get a lot of information you can use about each Trading Assistant, including:

➤ Trading Assistant's eBay User ID

➤ Trading Assistant's real name

➤ Trading Assistant's feedback score

➤ Trading Assistant's city of residence

➤ Trading Assistant's state of residence

➤ Trading Assistant's distance from your location

➤ Trading Assistant's provided services

When you click on a Trading Assistant's eBay user ID, you get all the information you need to make an informed decision on whether or not to do business with this seller. This information includes the following:

➤ Whether the Trading Assistant is bonded

➤ The Trading Assistant's contact information

➤ The Trading Assistant's feedback score and percentage

➤ Hours of operation

➤ The type of items accepted

➤ A complete description of the Trading Assistant's services, fees, and terms

eBay Basics

Many Trading Assistants do their work as a full-time business; others are PowerSellers or top-rated sellers who branch out into the Trading Assistant Program to diversify their business.

When choosing a Trading Assistant, treat the process as seriously as you would if you were hiring a person to work for you. You certainly have access to enough information to make an informed decision:

➤ Member profile: Every eBayer has a member profile, so this is probably the first and easiest place to start.

➤ Trading Assistant profile: The Trading Assistant profile is a comprehensive view of the Trading Assistant and what he or she offers. The profile includes the type of items the Trading Assistant specializes in selling, the fees, and any other information that helps sell the Trading Assistant's services.

➤ Experience: Click on the Trading Assistant's member profile or Items for Sale to see what the seller has sold and if the seller has experience selling the type of items you want to sell.

➤ References: You can ask the Trading Assistant to supply references from past clients just as you would ask for references from a person being interviewed for a job.

➤ Feedback: Whether you're dealing with a Trading Assistant or regular eBay seller, view the feedback score, percentage, and buyers' feedback comments.

As with any interview process, it's important you ask the Trading Assistant some pertinent questions such as:

➤ What are your fees?

➤ Do the fees include eBay and PayPal fees?

➤ When do you expect your fees to be paid?

➤ When do you pay me?

➤ How long will it take for you to list my items?

➤ What are my items worth?

➤ What do you do if an item doesn't sell?

➤ Do you guarantee against any damages to items while in your possession?

➤ Do you handle buyers' questions and feedback?

Working with a Trading Assistant is more personal than doing business on the eBay website. You may actually end up doing repeat business with your chosen Trading Assistant and developing an ongoing relationship.

eBay Basics

The agreement between you and the Trading Assistant occurs outside of eBay's jurisdiction. eBay's only involvement is that it provides a directory in which Trading Assistants are listed. You must work out any problems that arise between you and a Trading Assistant.

Becoming a Trading Assistant

Imagine, selling items that you didn't have to buy and making a profit without any output of money. It is easy to see why many eBay Store owners add this feature to their repertoire. However, becoming a Trading Assistant is not as easy as registering an account on eBay. Due to the trust involved in bringing two complete strangers together, it takes more than a smile and a catchy description to join the Trading Assistant Program.

The following are the criteria:

➤ You must be a member in good standing

➤ You must have a feedback score of least 100 and a 98 percent positive rating

➤ You must sell ten items in a three-month period

eBay Basics

Being a Trading Assistant can supplement your eBay Store income, or it can be a standalone business. Depending on how you sell yourself, there is no limit on how many people can hire you as a Trading Assistant to sell their items.

To sign up to be a Trading Assistant, go to http://ebaytradingassistant.com/signup/ and follow the instructions.

Making Money as a Trading Assistant

When you meet the criteria listed above, you can be listed in the eBay directory of Trading Assistants. You can create a profile in the Trading Assistant Directory by signing up to be a Trading Assistant. You will have the ability to describe your specialties, fees, contact information, and drop-off hours (if you provide that service). When people search for Trading Assistants, your name will appear in the directory and if they like what they see in your profile, they will choose you to sell their items.

Making money as a Trading Assistant has advantages over being a regular eBay seller. Instead of having to search for items to sell and building an inventory, people provide you with inventory. Since the program is free, you have little to lose by giving this program a shot.

Registered eBay Drop-Off Location

As a Registered Drop-off Location, you are operating as a consignment store. A consignment store sells other people's goods for an agreed-upon percentage of the amount it was sold for. This is a good expansion upon the Trading Assistant concept in that there is a physical location for people to go to.

The following criteria must be met to be a registered eBay Drop-off Location:

> ➤ You must offer a staffed drop-off location with posted business hours.

> ➤ You must agree to abide by the codes of conduct as outlined in the Registered eBay Drop-Off Location User Agreement.

> ➤ You must carry comprehensive liability insurance and bonding.

Having a Registered eBay Drop-off Location is no simple matter. Renting or owning a brick-and-mortar store creates what an eBay Store owner usually doesn't have to worry about: overhead. Running a storefront is a big step and should not be taken lightly.

CHAPTER 16

eBay in a Nutshell

In This Chapter

➤ Basics

➤ Buying

➤ Selling

➤ Customer Service

In this chapter you will get a recap of everything we have covered throughout the book. Along with this summary is some additional information that can be classified as miscellaneous and thus did not fit neatly into any other chapter.

The eBay Basics

Registering on eBay allowed us to become full-fledged members. Signing in every time we log on is a security measure that we fully understand and appreciate after hearing the horror stories of identity theft.

Helpful Tip

Most all the information in this book is found in some form on eBay. eBay has a Learning Center and Knowledge base that you can access to find information on anything eBay. In many cases in this book you've been directed to eBay pages for more in-depth information, but if something isn't clear, search for the subject on eBay for further explanations.

Buying on eBay

Over the course of the book, we have been introduced to eBay's trademark: the auction. We have learned how to place bids for items and have been introduced to the practices of bidding wars and sniping.

You have learned some techniques and strategies, such as how to watch an item, gauge the intensity of competing bidders, and the in and outs of proxy bidding, to increase your chances of winning auctions. Here is some additional advice you may find useful:

➤ Deal with specific people when possible: Individuals appreciate the repeat business, they are more apt to trust you, and they are more apt to provide positive feedback when deserved.

➤ Create your own rules of thumb: An example of a rule is not to deal with a seller who has received negative feedback. Once you have a set of rules that works for you, don't veer from it without good reason.

➤ Never back out of a deal: If you have buyer's remorse, there are procedures to deal with that. Under no circumstances should you take it upon yourself to simply void the deal. You may be charged for the item anyway or even banned from eBay.

eBay Basics

When you can't find a solution to your problem, you can click Contact eBay. Click Call Us and you are given a phone number. If you're signed in, you may also get a one-time code that will take you straightaway to a customer service representative.

➤ Recon your competitors: During an auction, you can click on the bids to see the bidding history and list of bidders. This gives you a lot of information, including the number of times each person has bid on the item. Someone who has bid multiple times really wants the item, so you can recognize that bidder as your biggest competitor.

➤ Pay promptly: The faster you pay, the more likely you are to receive positive feedback.

Post-Auction

Take these steps when you win an auction to remain in good standing with the seller and eBay:

➤ Pay for your item right away: The sooner you pay, the better it will reflect on your feedback score.

➤ Inspect your item the moment you receive it: If it is electronic, ensure it works and that all parts are included. If it is a game, ensure it plays.

➤ Communicate with the seller: Let the seller know if anything is wrong; if nothing is wrong, it is good form to send a gracious e-mail thanking the seller for a smooth transaction.

➤ Send your feedback as soon as possible: This is much appreciated by the other party but more importantly, expediency in posting feedback makes a good impression.

Selling

Here is where your entrepreneurial skills kicks in. You learned more than enough to start selling on eBay, but eBay is huge, so not every facet of selling was covered. Here is additional information about selling on eBay that you may find useful:

➤ Build a good reputation: Sell everything you can, even if it is not in your inventory. The way to build a reputation is by making good transactions. The actual product is irrelevant when it comes to building feedback.

➤ Constantly work on your listing description: You are a salesperson and your listing description is your sales pitch. Continue honing, editing, and improving it.

➤ Make becoming a PowerSeller and then top-rated seller one of your goals: This means always communicate, always provide the item as described, ship immediately, and so on. It is easy to get on a buyer's bad side, so ensure that it never happens.

➤ Sell what you know: Open an eBay Store that primarily sells items you have some expertise in. If your forte is not electronics, don't sell electronics. The exception is if you dedicate time to learning about a category so you can successfully sell items in that category.

➤ Maintain your reputation: Once a store is running and you're doing well, don't relax and expect the store to run itself. Keep improving and keep up or improve the good reputation you already have. The success of your store depends on your determination.

Growing Your Business

Once you open your eBay Store, you will be on a path that goes beyond the pages of this book. You will become an expert in eBay with nothing more for me to teach you. However, there are a couple of steps you can take that I mentioned in the previous chapters, steps that can expand your business. But with this expansion comes myriad expenses, potential problems, major overhead, the need for more intricate bookkeeping. In essence, you will be creating a corporation. As a reminder, two of the steps you can are as follows:

> ➤ Be a Trading Assistant: Expand your business, but make sure you don't bite off more than you can chew. Adding Trading Assistant to your repertoire requires taking on more responsibility, but as with any business, an additional service opens up a whole new realm of money-making possibilities.

> ➤ Get a storefront. This step is the largest and requires a lot of planning. You are essentially opening up a business. The statistics of business failure is astonishing, so you must have a business plan and you must be sure of every single facet of your business before you even think about taking this leap.

eBay Customer Support

eBay is dedicated to making sure everyone has the best experience possible while on its site. The fourth main drop-down menu on the top right of most eBay pages is Customer Support. The menu provides links that take you to areas that help you with any possible problem. The links in the Customer Support menu are as follows:

> ➤ Customer Support

> ➤ Learning Center

> ➤ Resolution Center

> ➤ eBay University

Customer Support

Clicking Customer Support takes you to a page with three possible ways eBay can help you:

1. Find an answer: Here you can enter a keyword that pertains to your question or problem. eBay will show you a list of links to pages that it believes most will most likely address your issue. To the right of the list, eBay offers Related Help, which also appears as a result of the word you searched.

2. How-to videos: Currently in Beta, this tab offers videos that cover selling tips and how to manage your account. Often watching someone go through the steps has a bigger impact than reading about it.

Helpful Tip

One of the diciest issues on eBay is retracting, or cancelling, a bid. As you would expect, eBay has many rules that cover this issue. Go to http://pages.ebay.com/help/buy/bid-retract.html to learn more about the criteria that needs to be met for eBay to allow bid retractions.

3. Contact eBay: Before eBay directs you to someone who can help you with your problem or question, you're asked to choose a category in which you're having the issue: Buying, Selling, Account. Click on any one of those categories you will get a further breakdown your options within that category. If you still can't find your answer, eBay offers a way for you to contact a customer service representative.

Learning Center

The Learning Center is a large knowledge base/instructional area/help page. It employs the use of a search engine, the ease of frequently asked questions, member-to-member assistance, and so much more. If you have a question or are puzzled by some aspect of eBay, this is where you will find answers.

Resolution Center

Here is the place you hope you never have to go to. The Resolution Center helps settle disputes between buyer and seller. When you begin a dispute, eBay assigns a case number to it and conducts an internal investigation based on the statements of both parties, the listing, and any other pertinent information. When the investigation is complete, eBay issues a ruling, and while this ruling can be appealed, they are final and must be adhered to. The penalty for going against a dispute ruling could be as severe as having your account suspended indefinitely.

eBay University

This last link in the drop-down menu is essentially the same as the Learning Center link except eBay University can help you find classrooms in your area to learn about specific aspects or everything about eBay.

eBay Expressions

eBay University is like other universities in that it provides local classrooms and instructors to teach classes that you can attend to learn about eBay. Go to eBay University, scroll down to the category you'd like to learn more about, and click Find Classes in Your Neighborhood.

For those who want to build a business on eBay's shoulders, keep in mind that there is no one surefire way to build a successful business. As with any successful, legitimate business, it takes hard work, ingenuity, and dedication to succeed. Apply those attributes as you go about building and running your eBay store, and you're more than likely to succeed.

For those who merely want to dabble in buying and selling on eBay, keep in mind that it's important to follow the advice set forth here—you never know when the winds will change and you'll decide to take the next step and build your own eBay Store. Happy eBaying!

INDEX